# THINGS THE BRAND GURUS DON'T WANT YOU TO KNOW

## AUBREY MALDEN

Published by

Kejafa Knowledge Works
35 Piet Retief Avenue
Noordheuwel
Krugersdorp 1739
South Africa.
www.kejafa.com

Designed by Sharné Edworthy
sharneedworthy@gmail.com

Typeset in Century 11 pt
Wilpro Printers
37 Carp Drive
Kempton Park
011 973 3295
South Africa
ISBN-13: 978-0-9947174-9-8

*"R16 billion a year wasted on advertising! You're joking?"*

**BOOK THE AUTHOR TO SPEAK**

Of particular note is the author's breath-taking and insightful "Rockumentary," The Fred Factor, about and featuring Freddie Mercury, whom he studied with in London. This unique "Rockumentary," complete with stunning and revealing archive video footage, makes a massive impact at sales and marketing conferences and events.

For more information go to **aubreymalden.com** and click on the tab, The Fred Factor.

**WANT TO WIN NEW BUSINESS?**

Together with the Forensic Marketing team, the author has helped write and orchestrate winning new business pitches for advertising agencies and media agencies. The Forensic Marketing process includes a unique technique of profiling the business prospects so as to touch their hearts and heads, and finally win the pitch...

*Business won includes:-*

- An international brewing company
- An international cosmetic and beauty company
- A local FMCG beverage and snack products company
- An international investment fund managing company
- Two international automobile companies
- An international FMCG food, drinks and confectionary company
- A local, and a international consumer-care pharmaceutical company
- An international FMCG household products company
- An international pet-care company

**Contact aubrey@forensic.co.za**

# CONTENTS

Wim van Melick

*Amsterdam*

*Ex Member of the OgilvyOne Worldwide Board*

*Currently Director of Training & Development at Ogilvy*

Like the legendary David Ogilvy, Aubrey Malden is a writer and a teacher. They both observe, judge, learn and share, and they keep asking how others came up with advertising and communication ideas, how they evaluated ideas and how they applied ideas for a range of brands in a range of media. Both have the ability to 'share the secrets of the industry'. I would like to add: 'And do it with pride'.

Through his journey through the advertising and brand world, both national and international, Aubrey has gathered many awards, much wisdom and practical examples of what works and what doesn't. You cannot write a book like this when you are young. You must have lived through many situations, have experienced what worked well and what failed. Especially you must have felt the pain of failure. And the elation of success.

The list of professionals Aubrey has met in his life, and who have influenced his thinking in this book, is impressive.

The book is mandatory reading for management, in fact anyone who manages brands. The content of this book, which you will read with pleasure, within two nights, will make you money. No kidding. Advertising, or whatever form of marketing communication you plan, must be based on the brand. This book explains, in an understandable and practical way, what a brand is and how it can be constructed, marketed and monitored. Brands make better margins than just a product. And during a recession products die, while brands live on. That is why it is so important that consumers experience the same brand attributes, regardless of which medium they receive the message from, or in. So, in order to build a brand, the relative values and costs of all points of contact where consumers might meet your brand, must be understood and mastered.

You will find in this book the difference between advertising and other means of communication, like activation, direct marketing and of course, public relations - all of which can cut through the clutter of the thousands of commercial messges we are bombarded with every day. Money spent on brands therefore is an investment, not an expense.

The book has some very practical tools and checklists, but above all it has many examples, some of which are Aubrey's own work and other work and case-histories he has observed. I counted 150 tips and 33 case-histories, and of those case-histories 19 were about mediums other than costly advertising. So, this book can save you money as well!

In today's world you can no longer only send messages. You must engage your consumers. Wiser brands invite consumers to think with them - to get involved to a point where the consumer will positively answer the Ultimate Question: 'Would you recommend this brand?' People depend more and more on the recommendations of their social circuit: friends, and colleagues . 'It is time for honest marketing communication', claims Aubrey.

What about creativity? Creativity in marketing communication results from the brief. "Give me the freedom of a tightly defined brief", a famous New York creative director once said.

As a creative director you cannot start with a blank sheet of paper. You must be inspired. That's why communication agencies have invented the brief, in which you find insights and lots of relevant information to stimulate the imagination. Aubrey, as an ex creative director, gives you the facts behind an inspiring and nourishing brief.

And then, the moment ideas are presented. How do you judge the work? Believe me, it is not easy to judge ideas, but it helps if you know what to look for, and Aubrey explains how, in his own down-to-earth style.

You need an agency? So how do you find the right agency? One that is original; that provokes new thinking, is a change agent, has common sense, and has the experience to work on brands and respect the target audience. Again, Aubrey gives you some hot tips on how to find the right agency.

The world is digitalising. Yet research reveals a structural under-spending in digital marketing communication. Be it the web or the mobile phone, all new age media will benefit from the principles of implementing a 360° brand strategy. Principles like branding, value proposition, segmentation, and measurement. Principles of effective marketing communication are, and always will be, based on the values you will read in this first-class practical book. New tools and media will emerge over time, no doubt, but traditional principles will never disappear.

This professional book is a must-read for everybody who is responsible for the brand(s) of his or her company or organisation. Not only will you become a better professional, but you will make money too.

Wim van Melick

In films, the credits, the 'thank yous', always seem to go at the end of the film. Few people seem to stay to watch them roll up the screen though, do they? But in books, credits always seem to be at the beginning. I wonder why?

Perhaps books still have a touch of good old-fashioned manners about them. And perhaps you, the reader are curious to see the people who the author believes have made a contribution to the book.

I like it that way. So, here are my credits:

Some of them I've listed here may even be able to make a contribution to your business. I do hope so. I've given contact details, so if you need them, here they are, in blue.

First I must thank Clive Simpkins, former colleague at then VZ Ogilvy & Mather. When I wanted to get more exposure at running marketing and advertising workshops he suggested I write a short article for a magazine. Upon receiving my draft article, he said, "This is not an article...this is the beginning of a book!" So, Clive, big hugs and thanks to you for the wise counsel and continuous encouragement.

Thank you to all at Ogilvy & Mather. Fred Lamparter, in New York, who helped train me and kindly rated me as one of the Top Twelve Ogilvy managers-to-be. To Robyn Putter, for whom I have tremendous respect, despite the fights along the way. You helped teach me to teach and manage, far more than you could ever understand.

To Peter Vundla (who went on to form Herdbuoys) and Gloria Mosia (now at Sonovision, gmosia@sonovision.co.za), who took me into Soweto, and the townships and shebeens, when whites feared to tread there.

And Bob Rightford, my CEO when Ogilvy was Ogilvy & Mather Rightford Searle-Tripp & Makin. Tough, demanding, honest to the point of bluntness, but at least you knew where you stood with Bob! A very passionate and committed man. I remember when, upon seeing him training for the Comrades, some board member said, "Oh, are you a jogger Bob?" "Jogger?" replied Bob, "Jogger?, I'm a fucking athlete!" Bob went onto run several Comrades and became high-up at Ogilvy & Mather international set-up. Bob was a winner in so many ways and a trailblazer in our industry.

Thank you too, to Brian Searle-Tripp, creative director of Ogilvy & Mather Rightford Searle Tripp & Makin. Brian was also one of the inspirational leaders behind The Red and Yellow School in Cape Town and spent some time with me and Bob, talking over a little of the pitch case-history of Volkswagen, featured in pages 103 and 104 of this book.

To the many directors, musicians, photographers and other technical experts I need to thank. The people who made my work come alive. People like film director Lynton Stephenson, who sadly passed away. A true gentleman who cast aside the often outrageous behaviour of others in favour of his quiet family life with wife Pippa and son Tarquin, two people whom I still cherish today. Lynton won a boxful of awards. A man without ego, he never boastfully hung them on the wall for all to drool over.

And then, the boisterous photographer Harry de Zitter. We seem to have followed each other around the world. Harry, where are you now? Miami, or Rome?

John Culverwell, of Sonovision, who added much to my radio commercials and deserves a share of the awards I have received.

Malcolm Miles, my chairman at McCann. Protective and encouraging me every step of the way in the early teetering and tottering days, when I was appointed CEO of McCann. Malcolm, taken from us when liver cancer struck him down. Malcolm mentored me. Supported me. I learned. When Malcolm died, he left a cavernous vacuum behind. Try as he might, Malcolm's successor couldn't hold a candle to Malcolm's charm, wisdom and wit. Talking about the importance of hiring the right staff Malcolm said, "It's hard to soar with eagles when you work with turkeys." Upon another occasion, when a board member was digging his heels in, Malcolm raised an eyebrow and gave the gentle retort, "Hey, why be difficult, when with a little effort you can be impossible."

Thank you Mark Fidelo, probably the best creative director I have had the pleasure of working with.

Karin Watling, originally with Ogilvy & Mather Rightford Searle-Tripp & Makin, who got me thoroughly involved with the Ogilvy Training Programmes. I have all the T-shirts to prove it, don't I Karin? And I have the joy and experience of running the workshops when I was lucky enough to score a 4.8 out of 5.0 from the Oglivy students who evaluated my performance (the highest of any of the facilitators). And now, under the auspices of our company, The Forensic Marketing Company, I hold a variety of workshops for advertising agencies, media independents and clients. Some of those workshops have helped make the basis of this book. Karin now runs her own HR Training and Human Resources company (khulisaframework@mweb.co.za). Karin is a star performer, is thoroughly dedicated, and diligent and will take your company to new heights.

John Tylee, the editor of *Campaign* magazine in the UK. Thanks for the exposure and support. Thank you Kay Blair and Gordon Young from the trade press in the UK.

Jeremy Maggs and John Farqhuar, here in South Africa, thank you for inviting me to share my thoughts with your listeners and readers.

Geoff Holliman from the London Marketing Society, who invited me to step up to the platform and the podium, and rub shoulders with some of the best marketers in the world.

Creenagh Lodge, Don Knight, and David Craton, of Craton Lodge and Knight. Together we built an awesome new product development company and along the way I learnt that understanding the consumer was the key to a brand's success. And I guess that is also where I learnt a tremendous amount about brands and how they interact with the consumer's thought and buying process, working with Cadbury, Bisto, Beecham, Mattel, Gallagher, McDougalls, Ski, Eden Vale and so on. I also learnt much about the value of packaging, and that the very form in which products are put has a negative or positive influence on the brand's persona and sales.

And Partrick Corr, of Corr Research. Innovative planner and researcher, who worked for the likes of Ford and Orange Cellular.

To Tim Bester and Barbara Cooke, who constantly open my and our clients' eyes to the delights and insights of Target Group Index (TGI), the research data base that any marketer worth their salt must get to know. See pages 240-242.

Of course there were many clients and many brands, but of particular note I would like to say thank you to:

Joe Beeston OBE, Ian Hall and Liz Breckendridge, of Highland Spring - the mineral water that bubbled out of the Ochil Hills in Scotland and that knocked Perrier off the number one slot in the UK (www.highland-spring.com). We cheekily called it 'The Scottish water the French drink'.

Alastair Mowat, Collin Wood, Brian Sharp, Willie Crawshay and John Griffiths from Scottish Courage, who taught me much about beer and in return we increased the sales of all the brands we worked on. And we broke the rules too, inventing new promotions, most of which worked to startling effect, including one that had sales increasing by 496%. There were, however, some serious malredemptions. Lesson learnt, test new promotions first. Thank goodness we did.

Simon Theakston (also involved with Scottish Courage) from T & R Theakston Ales. If you are ever in North Yorkshire, visit their brewery in Masham. Nothing beats the velvety smooth texture of Old Peculier, other than the knock on the head after a couple of pints (www.theakstons.co.uk).

Lord Jamie Sempill, formally from SAB. Later we worked together at Scottish Courage. Jamie has charm coupled with the infirmity of speaking quite bluntly to colleagues, irrespective of seniority. Consequently hot water was something Jamie became fully immersed in!

Michele Vincent, who invited me to contribute to the forward thinking of the Scottish Courage think tank.

Tony van Kraligan from SAB-Miller.

Sir Jackie Stewart, three time Formula 1 Grand Prix world champion. Jackie moved smoothly from the rigours of the racetrack into a first-class international business career, maintaining long-term relationships with a number of global brands, including Rolex, Ford and Moët & Chandon. Jackie would be my first choice if you ever wanted a motivational speaker. He taught me a lot about teamwork and has impeccable business manners. He has incredible mind-management and moves from one issue to the next with consummate ease. His book, *Winning is Not Enough*, should be read by all business people. The book even contains a Visual Book

Enhancement (VIBE) a DVD that breaks new ground in autobiographies, containing archive footage and interviews with Jackie, his son Paul, Sean Connery, Sir Martin Sorrell, David Coulthard and more (www.sirjackiestewart.com). The VIBE was produced by Jackie's other son Mark Stewart, from Mark Stewart Productions (MSP), his production company that has a strong reputation for first-class documentary making, from sport to archaeology. The programmes are broadcast all over the world on channels including Discovery and National Geographic (www.markstewartproductions.com).

Bill Marshall, formerly from Nestlé, who now owns, with his wife Margie, Syndicate Graphics, a packaging design company. A passionate professional (Bill@SyndicateGraphics.co.za).

Thanks to Brenda Koorneef, at Tiger. We worked together at Unilever along with the entrepreneurial Dave Jennens.

Another passionate man: Derek Carstens. I ran a lot of this book past Derek and his input was of paramount importance. Particularly for the section on choosing an agency. For he has been both poacher and gamekeeper. First he spent many years at Ogilvy, working his way around the globe, and then FirstRand, the country's largest financial services group, as brand director where he looked after such brands as Rand Merchant Bank, First National Bank, WesBank and Momentum.

Alan Main (originally at Roche and now Senior Vice-President and Head of Europe at Bayer Consumer Health), thank you for giving me the opportunity to use the Brand Triangle (see page 35 of this book), to reinvigorate Zam-Buk and grow it around 20% per annum, and in doing so turn it into the iconic brand it is today. It sure is 'The Real Makoya!'

To John Griffin, my partner at The Forensic Marketing Company. Thanks for the research, and the bags of fun that make every day, at 'The Office' a rare delight for staff and clients alike. (john@forensic.co.za)

And David Ogilvy. Thank you for 'letting me go' from my creative director's job in Europe. If it wasn't for you, and my meddling with the WWF and Sir Paul McCartney, I wouldn't have landed here in South Africa where I met and married the most complete wife a man could ever have. Ronnie. I love you and thank you for all you have taught me. You are not only the warmest of wives, you are a great art director. Patient with your 'babies' at JWT, and they all admire you. And patient with me, when we first worked together at Ogilvy and then later, when we pulled some rabbits out of the hat to help make two lack-lustre agencies begin to shine. You made my work look great and today, you never blow your own horn or polish your ego by trumpeting about the stack of London and international awards you've earned. For a German, you are unusually quiet!

Finally, a lot of people have helped me in my career but, in particular here, I have focused on those who have helped me, either through consultation, or just osmosis, to put this book together. I do hope that I have remembered to thank everyone. A difficult and onerous task. So, massive apologies to those whom I may have forgotten somehow.

# INTRODUCTION

# WELCOME

I was a late developer. Both in school and in advertising. Whilst others carried off the silverware I won just one advertising award in my first few years in the advertising business. But as I got older, I began, through being elevated to positions of management, to have to teach those agency staff below me and those clients who attended the training sessions as well.

*At the age of thirteen I had a passion for history. A passion which made me very curious about people. The make-up of their characters and motivations. It lead me to see how people interact with advertising and communication and I was lucky enough to attend one of the best advertising and marketing schools in London.*

And I learnt not to teach from the pulpit, but from the trenches. And it thrilled me. Because I taught myself what worked and how, and those below me seemed to like what I said. More importantly, their work got better. And so did mine! So, I got wiser and won more and more awards. Many creative awards, but the pinnacle was all the effectiveness awards. Ones that

I won. And those that those around me won as well.

I had learned to share.

When I started out I was amazed at the secrecy of my colleagues. I would ask them how they came up with ideas. How they evaluated them. How they sold them to our clients. Some shut their doors literally, so I couldn't take a peak.

I was also amazed how much bullshit seemed to surround the industry. When it was really a lot of common sense. A touch of logic with a sprinkling of magic.

In writing this book I was told by some in our industry that another book on brands and advertising and marketing techniques, was like another grain of sand on the beach. No one would want it. See it. Or read it. There were truckloads of books about advertising and marketing. And, of course, they were right. I rewound what I had read, seen, or attempted to read over the years. Big books. Some with tables, graphs, plans, checklists, processes, procedures, more checklists, and fancy techniques. In one book, lying dormant on our bookshelf at home, there are 101 charts and tables in a book of 198 pages.

There were the prosaic titles too. Alchemy and processes, even suns, moons and drawings of the planets (I kid you not) that Merlin would be proud of, and that agencies and researchers could charge clients a lot of dosh for interpreting as well.

I hope this is not such a book. It should be an easy, practical read. I hope it will save you, the reader, a lot of dosh and make a lot of money for you too. I hope it will stop you being ripped off by those black art gurus and I hope it will stop you ripping yourself, or your company off, through bad judgement, subjective opinion, or peer pressure.

The advice comes from my heart and head. From my observations and real experiences. Experiences that have made large amounts of money for my clients, and some experiences where, through failure, I have learnt the hard way, and been fortunate enough that the client has forgiven me!

May you avoid learning the hard way. And may you avoid those brand gurus who pedal their costly and vacuous wares.

# BRANDING

IT'S ALL TOO MUCH! GIVE ME THE SIMPLICITY OF BRANDS!

In an age of more products, information overload, and more commercial messages (in South Africa alone we have over 70 channels of TV, over 120 radio stations, and receive over 1062 commercial messages a day. In 2000 we had 480 consumer magazines, now we have over 670. We had over 260 community papers and magazines, now we have over 425) real brands make people's lives easier. They make the recipient's life easier, as they feel comfortable with the choice that has been made for them (or they have made for themselves) and they make the client's life easier, as their target audience is already predisposed towards the brand and understands what it has to offer them, both emotionally and rationally.

*"Not the Hugo Boss?"*

*The paperclip. A brilliant Norwegian invention. The precise bending of the wire makes it a tool that connects. And, it's amazingly simple, just like good advertising. (Incidentally, the Norwegians wore the paperclip in their lapels during the time that Germany occupied Norway in the Second World War. This simple twist of metal became a sign of unity, showing the Norwegians were bound together against the oppressor).*

Why should they care about your brand? The fact is, they don't. They care for themselves, their family, their friends, their pets, or earning a living and climbing the social ladder.

So we are wrong if we think the only competition to our brand is competitive brands; the competition is life as well! And life, in many ways, is far more interesting and often more time-consuming than a brand.

So, unless we make or help them care, we will not be on their radar. Unless we make our brand relevant to their needs and their environment, and contextualising it within the world in which the target audience lives and works, in short by positioning it and turning it into a real brand, one that is emotionally and rationally accepted, and consumed by them, we will fail.

*"Clothes make the man. Naked people have little or no influence on society."* - Mark Twain

## WHAT IS A BRAND?

A brand is built by dressing a product in a relevant and consistent suit of clothes.

Brands are 'planted' patterns in the brain. These brand 'patterns' instantly decoded, can mean 'trust-worthy, safe, strong, reliable, well-engineered,' and so forth.

Your target markets' brains are already wired to detect brand patterns. In an age of information overload brands are quickly sorted by the brain.

They allow instant buying decisions and acceptance. The brain works quickly to sort the familiar patterns. Over the page is an example of how your brain can read a pattern....

"Aoccdrnig to rscheearch at an Elingsh uinervtisy, it deosn't mttaer in waht oredr the ltteers in a wrod are, the olny iprmoatnt tihng is taht the frist and lsat ltteer is at the rghit pclae. The rset can be a toatl mses and you can sitll raed it wouthit porbelm. Tihs is bcuseae we do not raed ervey lteter by it slef but the wrod as a wlohe. Lkie a cdoe or prodcut we mghit konw!"

## HOW CAN YOU CONSTRUCT A HEALTHY BRAND?

You don't have to flounder around to construct a brand, or indeed, to reshape or breathe new life into an existing brand. The good news is psychologists have unraveled the 'millisecond' when consumers consider a brand, and the 'suit of clothes' that we spoke about earlier is a triangle! The triangle is instantly and subconsciously evaluated by the consumer every time a brand is under consideration. By understanding the three corners, or pillars of the triangle and how your brand stacks up against this subconscious customer criteria, you can build or maintain a healthy brand.

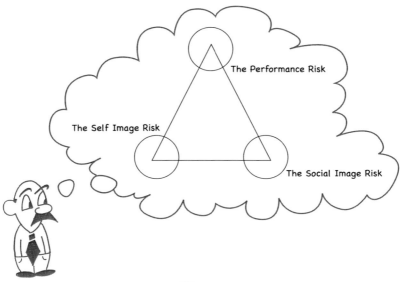

## THE THREE PILLARS OF CONSIDERATION ARE

**1. The Performance Risk** - Does the brand do what the customer wants it to do? E.g. If it's a deodorant, does it keep me dry? If it's a car, will it get me from A to B, comfortably?

**2. The Self Image Risk** - Will the customer enjoy the brand? E.g. If it's a deodorant, will I feel good putting it on; does it smell good? If it's a car, will I feel good owning/driving it?

**3. The Social Image Risk** - What will the customers friend's think if they see the brand? E.g. If it's a deodorant, what will the friends think if they see it on my bathroom shelf? Or, if it's a car, how will my friends feel towards the car, and in particular, towards me owning/driving that particular car?

You can see from the above that two of the criteria are about emotional values, Self and Social Image Risk, while only one is about rational values.

Try the triangle out yourself to see how it works. Choose a brand you know, or try evaluating BMW and Axe. See how robust BMW is on all three pillars (compared to, at the other end of the spectrum, the new Chinese and Indian cars) and Axe is, compared to an no-name brand deodorant, for example.

## A **LOGO** IS NOT A BRAND

While consistent use of colours, corporate identity and logo help build brand recognition, in itself, a logo is just that, a logo - the 'flag' or 'signature' that signals the brand's presence. For that reason the logo must be used in a consistent and recognisable manner, wherever it appears, from letterheads to laptop presentations.

Unfortunately when some people say, "I want more branding", what they actually mean is, "Give me a bigger logo." This is rubbish and this understanding debases the meaning of a brand.

# A  IS FAR MORE THAN A LOGO

Nike, BMW, Mercedes, Levi, Woolworths, and even Manchester United (yep, they are a brand with over 333 million supporters worldwide) have all been given meaning by consistent presentation of their logo or badge, but surrounding it has been the same suit of clothes (the verbal and non-verbal), the same tone, manner and style over many years. The vocabulary a brand owner uses, consistently, over time, builds the brand and the values. That is why to create a true brand you must look upon presenting, or representing, your product or service in a consistent style and tone, not in a subjective choice or whim, but as a business and commercial imperative.

## THE VALUE OF TIME

Consumers, over time, get to know a brand and move from being 'unfamiliar' with it (and sometimes hostile towards it), to 'familiar' with it.

The graph below, often used to show how brands can build a relationship with the target audience using Customer Relationship Management, demonstrates this simple principle.

### *The Time Factor*

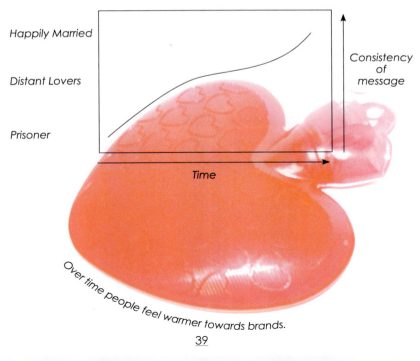

Happily Married

Distant Lovers

Prisoner

Consistency
of
message

Time

*Over time people feel warmer towards brands.*

## RECOGNISING THE USE OF THE ICEBERG EFFECT TO BUILD A BRAND

Although advertising agencies may not want you to believe this, it is not true to believe that advertising is the only way to implant brand 'patterns' (and the values of a brand) into your target audience's brain. Every day consumers receive brand values in other ways. This is known as the 'Iceberg Effect'. It is highly cost-effective, but requires that in every level of communication, internal and external (even sometimes the most obscure), there is absolute consistency in presentation, in the written words, the spoken words, the use of the logo, and the tone and manner in which you or your staff act and perform on behalf of the company.

In short, 'The same suit of clothes everywhere.'

The Iceberg Effect is defined as:

'The-below-the-surface attributes that get attached to a brand, either negative or positive.'

*What are the hidden mediums that can corrupt or raise the value of your brand? Your receptionist? Your lack of service? Your building?*

Frequently I walk past a fish restaurant where I live; there is always a stench of fish that pervades the area. We never eat in that restaurant. The tummy-turning smell tells my brain that that restaurant is unhygienic and probably serves rotten fish as well. That's an example of the Iceberg Effect.

Other retailers use smell and aroma to attract customers. The smell of freshly ground coffee in supermarkets and coffee houses is an idea that's been used for years. More recently sophisticated retailers, such as, fashion and furniture stores, use tiny amounts of complex fragrances in the air-conditioning systems to excite or calm the shopper.

Here are a few simpler ways that you can ensure you are building your brand, using the Iceberg Effect:

- The way your brochure is written and laid out.
- The style of promotion you may run and the type of prizes you may give for consumer or trade competitions.
- The consistent language you use to describe the product or service.
- The appearance of your building, inside and outside.

- What staff feel, understand and say about your product or service.

- What local communities believe and say about you.

- The consistent tone, style and layout of your trade presentations.

- The way you may use corporate entertainment to promote your company; the type of golf days or celebrations you may hold and the type of prizes you may give.

- How you work with, avoid, or embrace the media.

- Your signage and corporate gifts.

- The speed and style you use when reacting to an external enquiry.

All of the above require thought and time. How many golf days have you been to where it is just another corporate golf day? The same as anyone else's? Where is the brand character in the golf day? If you must do golf, do it differently!

*One aspect of your communication can*
*make the whole brand stink!*

## WHAT HAVE YOU DONE TO ENSURE CONSISTENCY?

Below is a simple checklist, by no means complete, that can help to ensure consistency in building and maintaining your brand and its values:

1. Is there an internal Corporate Identity Manual?

2. Have staff have been selected and trained to represent the company to the public media?

3. Have you a Media Book, which acts as a guideline for your selected media spokespeople? The Media Book should contain the choice of vocabulary and keywords used to describe your company, its products services and goals, to an 'outside' audience. The Media Book should avoid jargon, which is an encumbrance to the comprehension and acceptance of any brand.

4. Are your business cards and stationery a real expression of what your company stands for?

5. Have all laptop and DVD presentations been reviewed, and where needed, re-written and designed to fall in line with corporate guidelines and brand personality?

*"According to the theory of aerodynamics, and as may be readily demonstrated by means of a wind tunnel, the bumblebee is unable to fly. This is because the size, weight and shape of its body in relation to the total wingspan makes flight impossible. But the bumblebee, being ignorant of these scientific facts and possessing considerable determination, does fly... and makes a little honey, too."*

ANN THOMAS

AWARDS CO-ORDINATOR

THE BRAND BUILDING  15 SLOANE STREET  BRYANSTON
PO BOX 69765  BRYANSTON 2021
TELEPHONE (011) 709-6600  DIRECT LINE (011) 709-6732
CELL 083 561 7849
E-MAIL ann.thomas@ogilvy.co.za

OGILVY & MATHER RIGHTFORD SEARLE-TRIPP & MAKIN (GTG) (PTY) LTD

*Remember, business cards weren't originally 'business cards'. They were called 'calling cards'. They could say a lot about the company and make people enquire about the brand. The card above shows the clever use of a symbol to convey a philosophy. A philosophy, below, that drove this advertising agency to become one of the best in the world.*

yoga teacher

082 460 0648 · 011 485 2520

*Who said business cards have to be flat? No-one! Witness this folding business card that demostrates the flexibility of this yoga teacher.*

desireé fletcher

yoga teac

082 460 0648 · 011 4

desireé fletcher

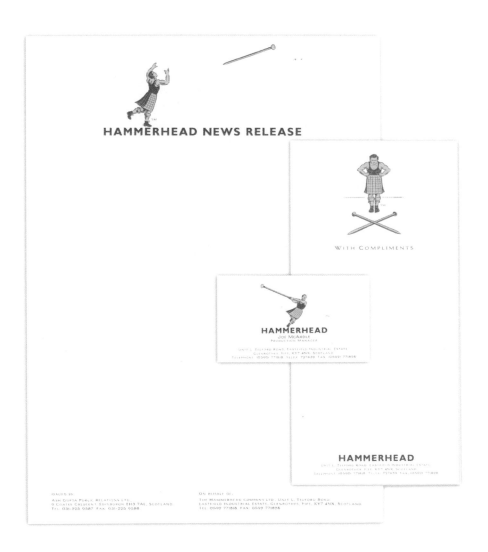

Even nail companies can make an impact through their corporate identity, as did this Scottish manufacturer of nails. Don't forget the smallest of details. Even the paper that is chosen can reflect the feeling of the company. If you could touch the paper that this stationery was printed on you would feel a fine texture that reflects the engineering nature of the company.

Remember, business cards are sometimes the first introduction to a brand, and they should immediately reflect the character of the brand - like this card in the shape of a razor blade, reflecting the character of this cutting-edge Sandton attorney.

6. If you have a transport fleet what is it that you have done to make it different, to reflect your brand? To be noticed? Edinburgh Zoo has a transit van with a massive rhino horn exiting the roof and the metal torn back, as though there were a wild rhino on board. You can't miss it. And in Edinburgh, rhinos make the news!

A small dairy in Scotland, Robert Wiseman Dairies, founded in 1947, originally delivered milk by horse and cart with the milk packed in glass bottles. On Robert Wiseman Senior's 60th birthday he handed on this business to sons Alan and Robert. By then they had a small fleet of trucks and a thirst for growth but no money for 'advertising.' So, they used the trucks. They painted them with the pattern of a Friesian cow. The trucks made a huge impact in the high street and on the motorways. People smiled when they saw them. The brothers then put the same pattern on their milk cartons in the shops and supermarkets. People bought their milk. Lots of it. So the business grew. They bought more dairies, and more distribution and more people smiled, and bought their milk, and their cream. In 1994 they floated on the London Stock Exchange. In 2001 their turnover was £300 million and net assets over £71 million. In 2007 their turnover had more than doubled to £605 million and net assets to £140 million.

*The Wiseman trucks turned the heads of the public and excited the London Stock Exchange and literally creamed the market.*

Simple things can make a great brand. As they say, '2+2=5'

## BRANDS MAKE MONEY

Accountants, those most cynical of the marketing business, now love brands:

• Brands are thrivers and survivors. While products die during recession, brands live on.

• Brands make better margins than just a product; accountants value them and pay 25% more in take-over deals for companies that own brands.

• Brands survive take-overs. Nestlé, those astute Swiss accountants, now own Kit Kat and they haven't changed the name of Kit Kat. SAB owns Miller and the Miller name has remained. Proctor and Gamble owns Polo and Hugo Boss, and has kept the names. The Russians own Chelsea Football Club, the Americans own Manchester United, and the names haven't changed. Long after the owners sell up, the brand name will remain and be worth a fortune too. (Incidentally, not only do they attract the public - these football club brands attract the top players too...who in turn attract the public, which generates the income and makes Manchester United the richest football club in the world, with more supporters in Soweto than can fit into Manchester United's ground, Old Trafford. And recently made a profit of £60 million!)

• At the recruitment level, brands attract talent. Who wants to work for Apple, for Sony, for Virgin, Mercedes, BMW, Levis? Hey, I do! How about you?

• And brands can be people too. You can earn more money (millions of $US) if you are a brand. See 'Can people become brands?' later in this book.

*not that kind!*

# THE BRIEF

I wasn't going to include this section at all, as it seems so obvious to those of us in the industry.

So, if you know what a brief is, and more importantly, how to write one properly, turn the next few pages and ignore this section.

Still with me? Well, you are not alone, for I have been asked many times by quite senior people to send them this simple briefing format, to help them get their thinking right when briefing out their requirements for new communications work. (Incidentally, you can also use this basic format to think through how you can pitch for business, run a political campaign, get ready for a hostile media interview, and indeed, prepare yourself for a job interview. Just replace, in your thinking, the name of the brand, with the individuals that you need to appeal to and that are going to interview you).

You must have a brief to enable you to brief out the work to an advertising agency, public relations company, or design or packaging company. And the brief is also an objective yardstick against which to measure the communications work when you review the proposals.

Rewrite the brief until you and your colleagues believe it really is a nourishing and stimulating one that can help catapult the brand forward.

It's not just a simple bit of form filling. It should take time and considerable thought. Not only about what you say, but also how you say it. Every word counts.

A tip here is to get your best writer to write the brief. The better the brief, the better the outcome. The brief should be no more than a page and a half of A4.

## 1. THE BACKGROUND

This should include a brief description of the brand and summary of the brand's history, mentioning the role it plays in the consumer's life, where it is today, what the problems are, and what the dynamics of the marketplace are, including any particular issues that concern you. If you have any research, include a summary here.

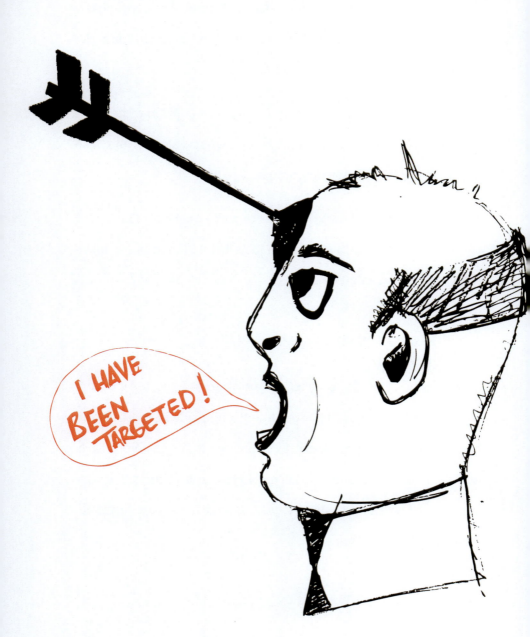

## 2. WHO IS THE TARGET AUDIENCE, EXACTLY?

This section should include a description of who you believe the target audience is for the brand. It should include who actually buys the brand and who actually consumes it; for example, wives usually buy men's deodorants for their husbands, but the brand choice is often the husband's. Holidays are often chosen by the wife, but paid for by the husband. The main consumer of Red Bull is not, as you may expect, the 16 to 25-year-olds but 35 to 45-year-old males, working hard, long hours, supporting a family, tired. They need a pick-me-up and they have the disposable income to buy lots of it. Sure the 16 to 25-year-olds buy it, but not in the quantity the 35 to 45-year-olds do.

Use language here that paints a picture of the target audience. Add thoughts and insights about what other products they may buy, what car they are likely to drive, where they might live, their likes and dislikes.

State age, sex, and Socio-Economic Level.

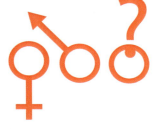

## 3. WHAT IS THE COMPETITION?

Although the answer here may seem obvious, it isn't always. The competition to a car brand may be another car, but it could also be an overseas trip for the family. Or a new swimming pool.

The competition to a beer could be another beer, or a cooldrink, or a glass of wine. That's why SAB won't have an agency with any other drink as a client.

## 4. WHAT IS THE TARGET AUDIENCE'S PRESENT ATTITUDE & PERCEPTION TOWARDS THE MARKET AND YOUR BRAND IN PARTICULAR?

Here it helps if you use quotes, as though the consumer is actually saying it, either verbatim from research, or from your own staff's observations. Using the words the consumer would actually use, not only helps paint a portrait of your audience; it also helps point the creative work in a direction that uses a 'tone and manner' that will engage the target audience.

Here is an example from an IBM briefing that was used to invite top managers to an IT conference:

"IBM? A big company we do business with. I don't deal with them personally, my IT man does. But I'm getting more and more involved now. As MD I have to. So much money goes into IT today, I need to get a grip on this technology thing. But it's all gobbledygook to me and companies seem to be getting out of their depth. I don't know who to turn to. I need to understand more. I am not a 'propeller head' but the buck stops with me."

*The invitation to the IBM seminar was an A3 map, that asked the invitees were they, 'In the Dwang', 'Up the Creek', or in, 'Clueless Close'. The answer was, many a recipient agreed, so much so that IBM had a packed and thankful house.*

From this 'intelligence' we clearly understood that these captains of industry were not IT-literate and were concerned that IT was getting ahead of them. The final brief inspired an unusual invitation, a spoof ordinance survey map that asked the recipients were they 'here', or 'here', or 'here'. With roads and cul-de-sacs with such names as 'In the Dwang' and 'Up the Creek' and 'Dead End'. They identified with themselves being in this position and IBM had three days of a packed house, and MDs thanking IBM for their plain-talking seminar.

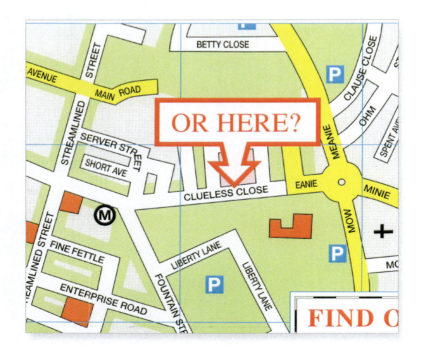

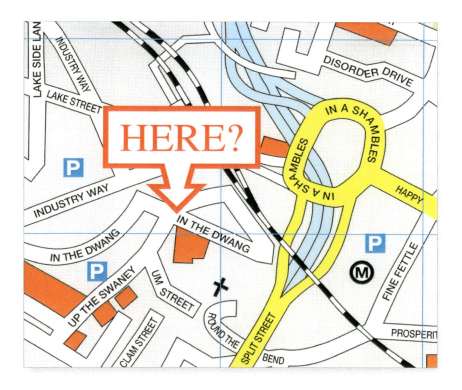

For a British savings scheme, The Scottish American Investment Trust (S.A.I.N.T.S.), we were briefed to recruit more shareholders for our client, fund managers Stewart Ivory and Company Limited, who offered a managed portfolio of UK shares and equity. We identified the target audience as those who were on the 'cusp' of investing in UK shares but didn't have the confidence to invest for themselves. Here's the attitude:

"Every day I see and hear about people making money from the stock exchange. I read about Rolls Royce shares making a packet. People buying Telecom shares and selling and making more. All these yuppies know what to do themselves, and the others have stockbrokers. I don't. I'm nervous about getting into something I don't understand. But I'm missing out."

We ran a quarter page advertisement in the newspapers. The headline read, "Buy the stock market for the Saintly sum of £25.00 a month".

Simple tone and style. It increased the shareholder base by 40%.

When the crash came, and people other than the SAINTS' shareholders dumped their individual shares, SAINTS, through careful fund management by Stewart Ivory and Company Limited, managed to weather the storm. In fact they saw the crash coming and divested a lot of company shares into cash. The results were good. We ran another advertisement, "Buy a Saintly peace of mind for £25.00 a month".

The SAINTS shareholder base increased again. Two lessons I learnt. Two motivators with regard to money and savings.

# "Fear and greed."

## 5. WHAT IS THE TARGET AUDIENCE'S DESIRED ATTITUDE AND PERCEPTION, HAVING SEEN THE NEW COMMUNICATION?

Here write down, again in quotes, the ideal response to having seen the new communication. In the case of IBM, it would have been something like:

"It seems to me that I am not the only one a little confused about what is happening in the IT marketplace. Thank goodness I am not alone. I'll get my PA to fill in the RSVP and see what these people at IBM have got to say. If I'm right, I should be able to understand the issues and see the way forward for the company and me."

## 6. WHAT REACTION DO WE WANT AS A RESULT OF THE NEW COMMUNICATION?

In this section you need to write down what you want to see happen as a result of someone consuming your message.

In the case of IBM it was 'register for the conference'.

In the case of car advertising it might be 'go and see the car', or 'ask for a test drive' or perhaps 'put the car on the mental shopping list'.

For a new beer, it might be 'try one the next time they visit the pub'. Or, 'pick up a six-pack next time in the bottle store'.

Not all work is done to attract new consumers either. A lot is invested in maintaining market share, or defending a purchase decision. In the early days of Toyota they suffered from credibility on all three corners of the Brand Triangle (see page 35) and were seen as a cheap alternative to the established European brands. The work we produced in Europe was to defend the buying decision of the Toyota owners and drivers. Our target reaction was something like 'the target audience will feel confident in their choice of a Toyota and be able to defend the decision in front of their friends'.

## 7. TONE, MANNER AND STYLE

Here we state what ideal tone and manner the brand should have. The way the brand should behave. Imagine the brand as a person. How should they behave to attract the target audience to look at them and identify with them and like them?

Too often in this section people write 'warm and friendly'. It seems a bit glib, especially when you consider, that by writing this down one might even consider the opposite 'cold and unfriendly'.

Tone and manner for a car could be, for Subaru, for example, 'Technical. Precise. Intelligent. Inspiring. For those in the know'.

For Newcastle Brown Ale when we launched it in the USA it was, 'Dark. Mysterious. Foreign. Charming and British'.

## 8. WHAT POSITIONING SHOULD THE BRAND HAVE?

This is a statement of the clear context and role that the brand will play in the consumer's life.

For Toyota, in those early days of brand development, it would have been, 'The reliable car that's excellent value for money'.

## 9. REASONS WHY

Here we put a list of ammunition that supports our positioning. Usually quite factual, but not always. Look upon this as an arsenal of information that can be used as support for the brand's claims.

For this reason this section is often known as 'Supporting Evidence'. Do not expect this list to be regurgitated in the advertising, though. If used, it needs to be dramatized selectively.

## 10. BUDGET

This is self explanatory, and refers to the figure you intend investing in this particular exercise of brand building.

# HOW TO KNOW IF YOUR ADVERTISING IS A FAILURE

## CAN YOU JUDGE WHAT IS GOOD ADVERTISING?

Before you answer that, let me tell you what happens when I ask that same question in the boardrooms of major advertising agencies and marketing companies. Out of 20 people, who create or approve billions of pounds', dollars' or rands' worth of advertising, about three in the 20 put up their hands!

So if you answered 'no', or 'not really', you are not alone!

But the fact is, you can. And they can. You all do it every day of your lives. Because, as a consumer, you are bombarded with advertising each day. And as it comes at you: via TV, radio, outdoor, newspaper, magazine, internet, MMS, and so forth - it engages you, or not, and you fend it off, or embrace it, or discard it as you go! And in doing so you are judging it.

So what's the problem?

The problem is as you sit in a boardroom you sit in artificial circumstances. A hothouse situation. You have prior information. You know, or should know, what the brief is (or perhaps you shouldn't...more of that later in this chapter). You know that the boss likes photographs (or perhaps you're the boss and don't like photographs!); others like product admiration, big logos, lots of words, and lots of colours. Green as opposed to red! Hell, I know some of this sounds quite silly, but think about it for a moment. I once had a client (the big boss and no-one in his organisation challenged him) who turned down the colour of a box carrying a direct marketing message because it was green! He hated green, because, we bothered to find out, it was the colour of the local opposition to the football team he supported!

We spent ages arguing with him. We had good sensible, logical and objective arguments. Eventually we won. And he did too, the response level was 36% (industry average, if there is such a thing, is around 2%), and the mailing paid for itself in new business within six weeks of the programme.

*WHAT IS YOUR PROBLEM?*

Then we had a client, who upon reviewing the creative work, which was advertising a chain of restaurants, insisted that we must show people eating his food and then smiling afterwards. The logic failed me. Was his food so bad that he needed to show people actually eating it? The fact was, people loved his big generous wholesome portions of food; we were briefed to show some of the more unexpected dishes he was about to put on the menu. What we were doing was showing the food 'up-close-and-personal' so delicious, I could have eaten it myself!

Another argument popped up too: the competitors showed people enjoying their food. This was not our argument as to why he shouldn't do the same to stand apart; it was his argument as to why we should do the same. Yep, and waste his money looking like everyone else! We could have used Sir Richard Branson in that meeting!

Differentiate or be doomed.

*Chuck enough money, for long enough and hard enough, behind bad advertising and it may eventually stick, just like wet spaghetti. Better approve work that will be recalled instantly, like the time when you grab hold of a burning match.*

## PRACTISE BEING NORMAL

So, what do you do to get your judgement going in the right direction? Be a real, 'normal' consumer.

If you are serious and have time, try this technique.

Put 100 random advertisements (not any of yours, otherwise this will colour the thinking) on the wall. Get your colleagues to look at them all for no more than 10 minutes in total (six seconds per advertisement; that's three times as long as researchers say consumers look at an advertisement before they engage or disengage with it). Then go round the room asking your colleagues to vote:

'GOOD, OR, BAD?'

Do not enter into debate. Just do it quickly, "Yes, or no, good, or bad?" Remember, you don't, when scanning a newspaper, turn to your spouse or lean over to your colleague in the next seat on board business class and ask them if it's a good or bad advertisement. Your brain does it for you. Your brain sorts it out. The wonderful computer it is, it 'trashes' it, or 'saves' it. The secret is to get your gut working, "Au naturel!"

As you go round the advertisements on the wall, rip all those that are not voted 'good' off the wall and chuck them onto the floor. Leave all those good ones on the wall (I did say 'good' and not 'brilliant', or 'award-winning' either). Be ruthless.

Now. Look at the wall.

First of all there will be a serious shock to the system. There will be around 15% to 20% of advertisements left on the wall. That's around 80% rubbish. That's not only true here in South Africa, but true in the States and Europe too. Believe me, I've done it. And in South Africa the figure on advertising media expenditure is around R20 billion, so that's R16 billion wasted per year. What's your company's contribution?

*Consumers' brains automatically discard the trash advertisements as they see them. Don't let yours be one of them.*

So how do we stop it? Easy. If only all of us did it.

First of all ask all those sitting round your table what made those 'good' ads on the wall. The answers tally with the normal list. The same list you get from advertising professionals (the same list we keep up our sleeves in case the attendees at these interactive sessions we hold don't come up with the answers, but they always do). Here are some of the pointers taken from a session:

## GOOD ADS

Simple

Uncomplicated/ Have one idea

Interesting

Involving

Have emotional appeal (make you laugh, smile, cry etc.)

Have a clear benefit

They stopped me/ looked different

Have class

## BAD ADS

Complicated

Cluttered

Confusing

Boring

Look the same as others

Not focused

Have no offer, or benefit

Messy

Unreadable

Don't touch you

Not engaging

Lack emotion

## KISS, KISS

The list is simple and what's more, most of the points focus on simplicity. That's why we use the mnemonic that you probably know, 'K.I.S.S.' as the title of these sessions, "Keep It Simple, Stupid" - or as one Japanese client rearranged it, "Keep It Stupid, Simple!"

Anyway, simplicity is the key. And that starts way before any advertisement is created. It starts right at the beginning. The brief. That has to be simple, clear, incisive, focused. If that is cluttered and long-winded and confusing how can it be distilled into a good advertisement? Too often, time and intelligence is not put aside for this process.

# "THE FIRST STEP IN THE JOURNEY IS THE MOST IMPORTANT."

*This Chinese proverb illustrates the importance of the very beginning of creating any form of brand building: getting the brief right!*

Some people, both clients and agency, can't put together a clear, single-minded brief. So they pile everything in, hoping that by default they have hit upon something. This is the shotgun approach and backside protector, all in one.

Others, particulary in the agencies, say of a precise brief, "It's too limiting." Isn't that exactly the point? It is a well thought through brief to set the work on the right road to woo the consumer. As Norman Berry, one of the worldwide heads of Ogilvy & Mather and later WPP, said:

**"Give me the freedom of a tightly defined brief."**

**HERE ARE SOME GUIDELINES:**

• Is it single-minded?

• Does it go from A to B? In other words, is it absolutely clear where the brand is now and what you want it to be and mean to the target audience in the future?

• Does the brief communicate who the target audience really is? Does it paint a clear picture of them? And please, psychographically, not just demographically. And please try not to use the outmoded, dusty and crusty LSMs we sometimes still seem to use in this country (a legacy of apartheid classification, meaning Living Standard Measurement). Consumers are not homes, as LSM classifies people; consumers are individuals, so use SELs (Socio-Economic Levels) and wonderful SEL data is available in this country from TGI (Target Group Index). Please note, if you have ever seen a LSM 7-10 aged 25 to 35, let me know! They simply don't exist. People do. So use SELs.

*LSMs are DEAD. Long live SELs (Socio-Economic Levels)!*

• Is the brief nourishing, stimulating and provocative? Is there an insight? Something that you can hang your hat on? A nugget about the consumer, the product, the different way it can be used?

• Is it human? What role does the brand really play in people's lives? A chocolate manufacturer may believe that their chocolate is something spectacular, that the consumer will really salivate over, when the reality is the consumer just pops it into their mouth for a sugar rush. Wham, it's gone in a flash. And in the greater scheme of things what on earth is the real significance of a chocolate bar in someone's 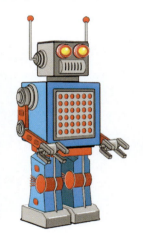 life? And, sorry OMO, is dirt really good in a South African rural home or on their child's shirt? In the first world yes…but here, well…er…no!

• What should happen *really*, as a result of the consumer reading the advertisement? And I mean *really*! Too often people think all ads are made to sell. Wrong. They are usually part of the selling process. So, what do you want the advertisement to do to the consumer? Get them to walk into a showroom and ask for a demonstration, or test drive? Get them to look you up on the web? Pick up a brochure? Welcome a rep? Prepare the ground for a future sale (put the brand on the consumer's subconscious shopping list so when they are ready to buy, they accept your brand on their mental shortlist - e.g. long-term insurance, a new car, a holiday home, or a GPS)? Remember, advertising is not an end in itself, but often part of the 'wooing' process. The sales force has its job to do, the store layout its job, the Point Of Sale its job and so forth. Or, indeed, the advertising might be there to motivate the consumer to buy your product, as is the case with a lot of FMCG brands.

• Have you allocated a production and media budget? Is it enough to do a proper job? If not, keep your money.

• Are the experts from your media planning and buying agency there? They are of paramount importance in the process; they are the people who will make sure that your message is in the right medium, at the right time, to reach your consumer.

• The advertising agency may create the advertising, but they are usually not media experts. The media people put down the right set of 'rails' for the 'train' (the message) to meet the consumer in the most relevant and cost-effective way. To test your media agency, ask to have a look at their media research. Even if they subscribe to some of the best planning and research tools, make sure they can use them. Just because you own a racing car doesn't mean you know how to drive it! And who wants to travel the road with someone who can kill you? Poor media planning and buying can waste a lot of your money, and help kill your brand too.

• Finally, well almost finally, where is the research? And I don't mean reams of it. Objective research with a simple clear pointer. It can be your own observations, which is in many instances much better than paying loads of loot for a kilo of paper! By the way, TGI can help you here again. They can map out the psychographics of your consumer. What they believe in. What makes them tick? What other products they use. (Do I have an interest in them? Absolutely! An interest that we don't waste money on bad advertising by guessing. Remember what David Ogilvy said on page 170).

• When that brief is ready, look at it again. Is it first class? No? Then write it again…and again.

Now, finally. Does it really have to be an advertisement that you may need? As the business imperative is ultimately to sell, would your money not be better invested in training the sales force to be able to sell better? Or in using a Customer Relationship Programme, or investing in Point of Sale, or running a viral or guerilla campaign? Keep your mind open when your advertising agency and media agency return with their recommendation/s. Don't be prescriptive with the choice of medium. Be judgemental in what business results you will get, instead.

## DOING IT ROUGHLY IS BEST

OK. So now you have given the brief and the idea is being presented to you. Ask for a 'rough' a sketched-out idea. Beware of bullshit - that's usually fully finished ideas with, for example, photography, and typesetting - the 'full computer-made enchilada'. Often bad ideas hide behind the glamour of a flashy finish. I rather like the Turkish proverb here, 'He looks like a rat with a gold tooth!' Beware of the flash!

A note here, about highly-finished computer-generated layouts, taken from Paul Arden, one of London's top executive creative directors who won a hatful of awards while he was at Saatchi and Saatchi:

*Rough ideas sell the idea better than polished ones.*

If you show a client a highly polished computer layout, he will probably reject it. If he doesn't like the face of the girl...or the trousers worn by the man on the right...he will reject it.

There is either too much to worry about, or not enough to worry about. They are equally bad.

He won't see the big idea.

# DOES IT MAKE YOUR PALMS SWEAT? ARE THEY UGLY? GOOD!

So now, here are some pointers in guiding your judgement when looking at the proposed advertisement:

**THE IDEA:**

• Does it  you?

• Does it make you laugh, cry, sweat, read on, or switch off? (In the days of the great ballsy advertising for Sales House, the client asked Ogilvy for "Advertising that will make our palms sweat." They got it and with it came the establishment of Sales House as a brand).

• Is there a visual or verbal burr? (Something strange or eye-catching, like a photograph that is mesmeric, a model that looks different to all other models you've seen in advertisements - they may even be ugly. Hey, ugly can be good. In the UK there's a model agency called Ugly, they specialise in ugly people, fat people, people with big bulbous noses, lazy and cross-eyed. Perhaps there's a headline that causes dissonance, like, 'This is a happy man' written under a picture of an unhappy man. Or a headline under a picture of a beautiful vibrant green valley, with a headline that says something like, 'What would you say if we were to dig up this valley and put a massive pipeline through it?' This was an advertisement for Shell and their nature conservation. The first line of copy went something like, 'We already have and we put the valley back together again...').

• Does it have story appeal? Is it involving you, making you enquire what is going on? For example, in a Range Rover advertisement there was an aerial view of a suspension bridge going across a frozen lake, with cars on both sides of the road. The headline reads, 'Can you spot the Range Rover in this picture?' Looking at the road and amongst the mass of motor vehicles all jammed up in the slop and slush of snow, no, I couldn't see it. Then I looked to the left of the bridge; I looked at the frozen lake, in the snow. And there they were, fresh, crisp tyre tracks, and at the end of them, yep, the Range Rover! Story told.

• Does it frighten you? Are you afraid it doesn't fit within the normal conventions of advertising (I don't mean, is it bad-mannered, no one buys from bad-mannered people) but is it unconventional, off the wall? Don't dismiss it. It could be just the job to get your brand noticed.

• Does it do what you want the advertising to do? (See next page, smelling a R.O.S.E.) Yep. Then blaze trails. Go for it.

• Will you remember it tomorrow? Is it sticking in your brain? If it is, that's good. If it isn't, go back to 'go' and start again.

• Is it in great danger of being read?

If you have misgivings about what you have seen, ask yourself, 'Does it do what we want it to do?' The operative word here is *do*. Advertising is not there to *say* things to consumers, it's there to *do* things to them - cut a coupon, take a test drive, try a brand, and so forth.

## SMELLING A R.O.S.E.

This is a simple technique you can apply when finally reviewing the advertisement. It works, and the mnemonic is easily remembered (I first introduced it to Steve Miller, who was then a brand manager at Unilever and was recently at AVI as brands director. When I hooked up with him, for the first time in over 20 years, he said, "I remember you, you're the guy who asked, do we smell a R.O.S.E.!") Here's how it works. Look at the advertisement and appraise it thus:

1. Is it Relevant?
2. Is it On Strategy? and is it
3. Excellent in its Execution?

If you are in advertising and you are reviewing the advertisement, or bevy of advertisements, to decide which one to present to the client, here are, I hope, a few helpful pointers:

**DO:**

• **Own the page.** Have a distinctive look - a personality sympathetic with the brand and your target audience. For example, are you to be bold, aggressive, informative, scientific, loud, soft, trendy, casual, orderly, classical, outrageous, courageous, small, etc.?

• **Let the idea lead the layout.** Is the idea working? Is the headline the main attractor, or the visual? Or a perfect balance and marriage of the two? Or is the design of the advertisement just too ornate and masking the idea?

• **Take out all the clutter.** Keep It Simple, Stupid. Ask yourself is it all needed? If it isn't don't put it in! (Art directors want pictures, writers want headlines and body copy. Clients want logos and pack shots. But are they really needed? Hey, there are no rules.)

• **Remember white space buys you readership.** It lets your advertisement and the content of your advertisement 'breathe' and be seen amongst a sea of wave upon wave of editorial and other advertising competing for a millisecond of attention in your consumer's overloaded brain. Ads, like life, shouldn't be complicated.

Beware of the client who counters, "I bought all that space and I want it filled up." Here's something that may illustrate the point. There are two identical large rooms. One is crammed full of furniture and pictures; you don't know where to sit, or look. The other room has just one chair and only one picture, the same priceless picture on the wall as the other room. You know where to sit. You know where to look. You are drawn there. White space draws attention to your creation.

## CRAFT YOUR ADVERTISING

When you are about to put the advertisement into production:

• Be objective; use the strategy to drive your decisions. Use reference material, photographs, swipe art, and other ads to give your client a feel of what you are going to create.

• Have a pre-production with your client. It's their money they are investing, make sure they understand where, how, and why their money is being invested. (Advertising is not a 'budget', it's an investment. I remember a client from Unilever admonishing an account director when she said, "…and your budget is…". He said, "Please never use that word again: it's 'investment' not 'budget'. We are investing in advertising, not spending." Splitting hairs, maybe? I think not. It's a great principle).

• If your advertisement looks like it has been made with care, so will your product/brand.

**DON'T**

• **Ever stop being a consumer.**

• **Settle for second best.** If the idea is no good, chuck it out.

As they say, "You can't polish a turd!"

## DON'T

- **Over-write or over-art direct an advertisement.** Less is more.

- **Skip the detail.**

- **Be dull.** People avoid dull people.

Finally, there will be occasions where clients or your boss, in the advertising agency, will turn the idea down, or ask for changes. Here are some thoughts on getting the work going again:

Make it a team effort. Share the problem. Discuss the solutions. Do it 'with and without Vaseline **✳**.' What this means is if a client or boss asks for changes, make those changes. It's their right. But make sure you understand what those changes are. The best word you can use in this business is "Why?" Asking "why?" will make them think through their objections and will help you understand them and find a route to the answer/s. Having made their changes, compare it to the original and make the changes that you, as an expert in your area, think are right. Then present and compare. Common sense usually prevails. However, as they say, "Common sense isn't that common!"

Good luck.

**✳**

See over for Vaseline

**＊ WITH AND WITHOUT VASELINE?**

*You may think this has some intentional sexual innuendo attached to it. Not true. This comes from the days when TV commercial directors and stills photographers put a very small smudge of Vaseline on their lenses to get that 'soft focus' feel, which made the picture look more romantic or like a flashback. Clients and agencies were a little unsure of the result so the poor cameraman was asked to shoot it both ways, 'with, and without Vaseline!'*

# CHOOSING AN AGENCY

It's a question of style and fit. A bit like buying a trustworthy pair of shoes. Just like there are many different shoe types and shops - the international, the boutique, the cut-price and the owner managed - the same exists amongst the plethora of advertising and communication agencies.

And just like there are those shoes that will be with you for a long time and remain true and trusted friends, there are shoes, and agencies, that are an uncomfortable fit, either from the outset, or as time moves on. They lose their initial shine and shape and become a waste of money, so you discard them and then you have to go out to shop again.

So, if you are serious about advertising, if your profits depend upon its effectiveness, it's your duty to seek out the very best people to work with you on your advertising and communication. If you see advertising and communication as an investment then you are serious. But if you see it merely as an expense, well, perhaps you are not. And maybe you should skip this section of the book completely.

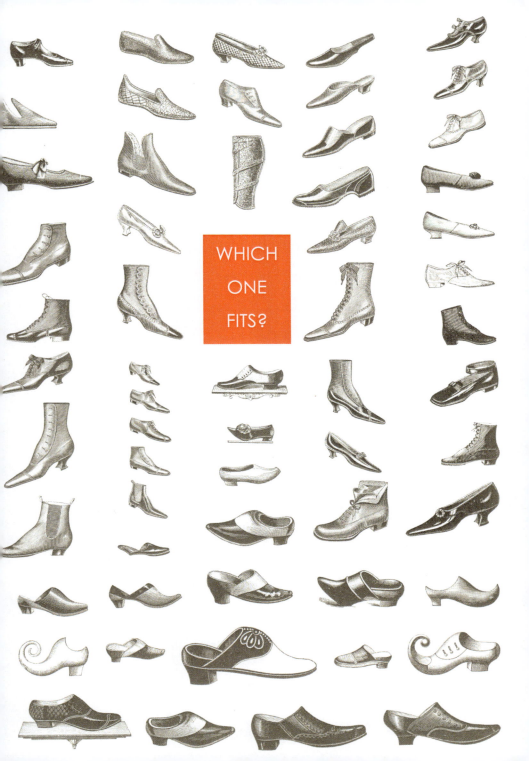

WHICH
ONE
FITS?

Anyway, the choice starts with you. And some soul searching. What do you want from an agency? Write down a list of attributes you want. If you have a fashionable brand maybe you need a fashionable agency? If it's a retail brand you have, that requires fast turnaround maybe it should be an agency that specialises in retail? If your business is stagnant look for an agency that has helped turn a business around. Look for one that has made a small client into a big one. Look for a new agency born out of an old agency. All styles exist.

Look for work that you like, in the magazines, newspapers, on television, on posters and find out the name of the agency, or agencies, whose work you admire. In many countries there are 'keylines' - a very small line of type that runs up the side, or along the bottom of the printed advertisement, which gives the name of the agency. Alternatively ring the publication or the advertiser and ask for the name of the agency.

Call them up. Or drop them a line. Ask for a meeting with their CEO and Creative Director and tell them what you are looking for and why. Ask them to present some of their best work, say four campaigns for different clients, and ask them to tell you a little about the work, and the problems the campaigns helped solve. Also ask them to tell you about any screw-ups that have been made or any key learning's they have made from a mistake in a campaign. Everyone makes mistakes, but not everyone is open and honest about it. I would suggest you want honesty from your communication partner?

Make sure the chemistry is good and if it is, then meet with their suggested team. Perhaps have dinner with them. Get them relaxed over a glass of wine. Loosen their tongues.

Test them and see how they behave. Do they constantly agree with you, even when you set them up and intentionally say stupid things? Are they business people? Do they ask you, and talk to you about business results, or do they just boastfully talk about ads and awards? Are they good listeners? Intellectually curious? Would you be happy for them to present to your board?

And again, did you like them? If you appoint them the relationship must be intimate and robust enough to talk 'open cards' all the time. If you have done this with a couple of agencies or so, then

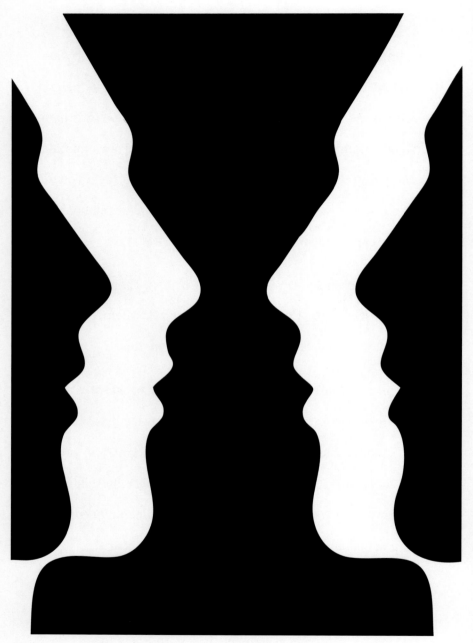

*When you visit an agency do you see people, or just wine. Or even better, both!*

make your choice. Don't haggle over price...well don't haggle too much then! Pay them well and you should get star treatment.

Brief them well, and don't keep a dog and bark yourself.

Volkswagen South Africa more or less took the above approach in 1979. They put six agencies on their shortlist, visited each one, and asked to meet the team that would actually work on their business. They asked for no creative work to be produced for them and no pitch. They looked at the work that the creative people had produced who would be working on their business, including work they had produced at other agencies. Particularly car work.

They had a score sheet where they marked each agency on a number of criteria: creative work, administration, financial stability, quality of staff, etc. Then they added up all the points and decided whom they would appoint. And the winner was... well, er, it wasn't the agency that had the most number of points. Because the agency that had the most number of points they decided they didn't actually like that much. The second agency was more vibrant, young, fresh and eager. The chemistry just seemed right, and so they appointed what was then Rightford, Searle-Tripp and Makin, Cape Town, the agency that is today Ogilvy. They still hold the business today, over 30 years later. It's one of the most rewarding and enduring relationships that the world of advertising has known.

And it's worth pausing a while to examine why. Many things added up. But chemistry won the day. And honesty. What Volkswagen met was what Volkswagen got. They met the eager and spirited senior people in the agency: Roger Makin, Brian Searle-Tripp and Bob Rightford.

And it was this team that worked tirelessly with the client. As Brian Searle-Tripp said, "There was no us and them. From the start it was a seamless relationship. Often the client used to pop into the agency late at night to see us reviewing our ideas. We worked hand-in-glove together. In fact, we worked like that with most of our clients."

The relationship has built Volkswagen and Audi into one of the strongest and most rewarding brands in the country.

Today, sadly, many people, both agencies and clients see the business as a 'service industry', where agencies dish up work to clients like members of the public order food from a menu.

Beware of new business teams and departments. They may be fine in helping to put a pitch together for your business but after that you will never see them again.

If you are looking in the UK you can go to the Advertising Agency Register, (www.aargroup.co.uk/). They have on their books a broad spectrum of communication agencies, including advertising, design groups, interactive and public relations. Each company has lodged with the AAR a portfolio of work, a credentials presentation and so on. You brief the AAR they then shortlist a small selection of companies that they believe match your brief and you go along to the AAR and privately and confidentially review the shortlist. It's a bit like using a headhunter to find a candidate to fit a particular job specification.

The AAR has offices in other countries too. At the time of writing this, there were a total of eight offices, including the USA, Singapore and Australia.

There is of course the á la carte route as well. If you feel, for example, that you don't need a full service agency, or you feel your budget won't stretch to pay for the full agency team, or maybe it's just a creative team you need to look after your business, then there are various routes you can take to find the right fit.

*Which way will you go?*

If you are really hungry for outstanding creative work don't be afraid of approaching a large agency with a great creative reputation. Agencies are hungry for awards, it raises their profile, inspires their staff, makes existing clients feel good, and attracts new staff. And it polishes the creative ego. In South Africa agencies actually get points for the awards they win and those points go towards their rating in the marketplace.

Many of the international agency groups rank and reward their CEOs and creative directors according to their ranking in their local marketplace. So, awards are a great carrot to many agencies. If this is the route you choose, make sure that you are honest about your budget and your aspirations about wanting award-winning work.

Furthermore, if it is award-winning work you're after and you have a small budget, often agencies will subsidise the cost of making the advertisements by not marking up any production costs, or doing a deal with their supplier by asking for the television commercial, radio, print advertisement etc, to be produced, 'As a favour'.

There is a lot of debate about awards in the industry. Are they good or bad? My feeling about awards is that, generally speaking, they are good for the industry. In my experience the advertising work that I or my teams have won awards for sells product exceptionally well, but we never set out to win an award, we set out to produce the best possible solution for our client. Where awards have got out of hand is where some agencies produce work primarily to win awards and pretend the work is for a legitimate client. This blatant cheating harms the industry and the client, who sometimes isn't even aware that it has happened.

If you are just looking for a creative team you can also avoid the whole agency thing by seeking out a top, or young and hungry team, to moonlight for you. Some agencies allow this. Others don't. Make sure you know what the situation is. Creative headhunters can also find these teams for you, for a fee. Or you can look for the advertisements you like, find the name of the agency that produced them and call the agency up and ask for the name of the individuals who did the work you admired.

Outsurance went the á la carte route. They hired the creative team who conceived the ideas. Then Outsurance found a production company to make the commercials and paid them directly.

There are many right ways to get the work that you need to help build your business. Like all good things, it starts with sitting down and working out what you want and why. Remember, though, the consequences if you are prone to dabbling and penny-pinching: **'if you think knowledge is expensive, try costing ignorance'**.

If you become a penny-pincher you will be known for it and avoided by the better professionals. The CEOs of all agencies more or less know each other and they do sometimes discuss clients and share views. I remember in the UK getting a call from a very large double-glazing company with a budget of around £20 million. Calling from his Rolls Royce (he made it clear to me he was in his Roller and not the Ferrari), he said he was just around the corner, was firing his old agency and was thinking of shortlisting us. Could he come in immediately and see me? I asked him to hang on for five minutes and I would call him back. I called a quick meeting with our head of client service that had worked with the incumbent agency. He told me again how this client had bullied the previous agency, and always penny-pinched, every step of the way. In fact he had two different agencies in the past three years.

I called Gerald, the potential client, back and said we had had a meeting and were unable to handle his business, "due to our vision for the future of our agency" (i.e. we didn't want our staff bullied and sworn at and be paid peanuts for the pleasure. 'Crap' was a word he used when looking at an advertisement the previous agency produced, which he tore up in the meeting. 'Shite' was another word he used liberally. We neither wanted to listen to this language nor do it for a margin so small that we couldn't care about what we produced for him).

Gerald, as I recall, swore at me and put the phone down. Five minutes later the CEO of one of our competitors called me and said he had just had a call from Gerald. "Are you going to see Gerald?" I asked. "What do you think? Do you think we are crazy? We are just working out how to say to him 'no thanks' gently!"

How can you go wrong with your appointment process? You can

put your business out to pitch. Some clients shotgun and put it out to six or more advertising agencies. That's lazy. If you must pitch, narrow it down by meeting and reviewing the existing work of a maximum of six and cut it down to a final three.

Beware, a pitch is exactly that. A one-off hit. The agency can be lucky or unlucky with its work. They can hit the nail on the head once. After that it's a miss every time. Or they could put an exceptional effort into the pitch and woo you with every bell and whistle in the book, and after that it's back to normality. So look for consistency in their work; look at their work for other clients. And do call their clients, very few prospects do.

Some clients, when they put work out to pitch, write a brief and just send it out. Laziness. Worse still, they refuse to answer any questions, or, on the other hand, share all questions and answers with all the pitching agencies, levelling the playing field. If one team plays better because they question better, then they should have the advantage. By sharing questions and answers you create an unnatural playing field and life's playing field does actually slope.

"Hey Rodney, this pitch slopes, that's not fair!"

"That's life Bertie!"

# TIME.

Clients take years to perfect their products and services and then give an agency sometimes as little as two weeks to put a pitch together. This not only shows disrespect for the product or service, but disrespect for the advertising investment as well.

Give agencies at least two months. And interact with them as much as you can during the process; you will learn a lot about physical chemistry and intellectual ability.

If an agency wins solely on price, you have a loser.

Don't unthinkingly frighten your agency with threatening to move the account. Frightened people run scared and lack confidence and are powerless to produce good and adventurous advertising. If you put the fear of God into your agency then you do yourself a disservice. The CEOs had a vote at McCann, when we were hypothetically conceiving the perfect agency, and the sign above the door would read 'No Fear'.

A long-term contract helps emancipate fear. It not only helps your agency work hard on your business; it also helps them spend less time looking at other business should your business go. On the other hand, it can create over-familiarity. Annual appraisals of agency and client performances help stop that and build closer and more open relationships.

# HEY, REAL BRANDS ARE BUILT BY MAVERICKS NOT INSTITUTIONS

It takes balls to build a brand and most balls don't belong to institutions. They normally belong to mavericks.

Sir Richard Branson is one. The entrepreneurial partners of Bluetongue Beers, bought by SAB Miller in Australia, are other examples. Even Charles Glass, the original brewer of Castle Lager is another. Henry Ford was another. Ben Filmalter, of Mugg & Bean's massive muffin fame is another.

For brands are born from a vision. Usually one person's vision. And usually they rock the boat. Mavericks.

Starting out, they don't read any weighty tomes on brand building. They don't spend tedious hours studying for an MBA.

What do they have in common? Common sense, and as we know, "Common sense isn't that common!"

## GET THE GUT, OR EMPLOY ONE

They love and understand people. They watch their behaviour. They smell trends before they happen. Some say they invent them. But they invent them because they have, first of all, a deep and intuitive understanding of what's happening. A good gut. They know what people want. They get their gut working. Spot a gap in the market, focus on what they need to do. And do it.

As Sir Richard Branson says about his lessons in life, "Screw it, Let's do it." In fact the media call him a 'maverick in paradise'.

These stars of brand builders have no reams of clichéd verbiage in their company vision. The lesson I learnt? Torture your vision. Take out any cliché. Focus it until it harnesses and guides everything that you and your staff do. Make no room for ambiguity. The best vision I have ever seen is from Ivor Tiffenbraun's at Linn Hi-Fi's headquarters in Scotland: 'Thrill people with sound'. That inescapable measuring stick measured everything his company did. His factory was a thrill to tour. His technology the very best. He demanded innovation in everything they did. He demanded and only approved radical and innovative brand-building advertising. How do I know that? My wife created it and it sold millions of hi-fis. From the hallowed halls of Harrods in London, to the bling Stores of LA.

HIS LIFE REVOLVES AROUND THE CITY. THE CLUB. AND A COTTAGE IN KENT. HE'S FAR TOO BUSY TO LISTEN TO A LINN HI-FI. HE'S THE MOST BORING OLD FART YOU'LL EVER MEET.

LINN HI-FI

How did she produce the ads? They were born out of Ivor's vision. They thrilled the target audience and upset those that weren't the target audience. He cared about one thing. Turn the target audience on and if you turn the conservative stick-in-the-mud audience off, who cares? And make sure you sell. And it did. And at R95,000 a pop to around R1.2m that's some real sound adrenalin rush you can hook your anvils up to!

Contrast that with a big corporate I worked for. They were so megalomaniacal and upset that the ads we were about to produce only appealed to 70% of the target audience. Hell, to have 70% of the target audience is no mean feat. And the brand? Axe. Which is doing very well now, thank you.

## STUCK IN A CORPORATE? THEN BUCK IT

So, if you are in a corporate, get out. Or lead it from within. But you will have to focus and fight to turn the ship around. I helped changed the face of a British university through the marketing and repositioning of the university student recruitment campaign.

But we couldn't have done it without the change agent within. The willing chancellor, Bernard. Eccentric. Argumentative. Fantastic to work with. We quite bluntly told the Chancellor that potential students didn't want the precious degrees his varsity or any of his competitors were offering. Instead we told him his potential students wanted employment. So, his precious varsity's degrees were branded as leading edge ways to get fantastic jobs around the world and in top-class professions and companies. The ads and their prospectus broke every rule in the book. We didn't use old dusty and crusty language. Or any pictures of musty mortar boarded professors and undergraduates. We showed the after study activities (you know what I mean). We didn't promote mechantronics, but the fact you would have the skills to make a full-size dinosaur walk! We didn't promote the legal degrees but the fact that you could solve multi-million-dollar deal-breaking contracts and, if you were smart, you could get a percentage of the deal too. It was stuff that had the students applying in their droves to the point that the varsity was very much over-subscribed, even in areas like science and engineering.

But we had to swim against a strong skeptical stream.

We, the chancellor and one member of his team, had to present to the whole skeptical group of professors who had more degrees and doctorates than mounds have termites. We persuaded them, against their better judgement. As our media director said, it was like being examined by 300 academics. So, we got the research we needed and prepared our pitch. We rehearsed every single argument we thought they could throw at us and practised our rebuffs. We were invited to pitch for two hours. They kept us for five hours. Question after question. Our media director was right, it was a test. And we got the job. When all university intakes were down by an average of 8% we increased our varsity's intake by a massive 25%.

Two years later we were fired. And that really did hurt. Not because the intake wasn't up again (it was, and we received a Marketing Effectiveness Award too) but because the termites found it difficult to stick to the strategy in everything we wanted doing. And other varsities began to become a little jealous too. And we fought back, which was tiring for all concerned. And our main client, the chancellor, was getting worn out with the constant internal bickering and battering. (Another lesson: building brands is not just about the ads you produce. It's the way your staff behave and believe. The way internal silos are dissembled. The way the building looks. The exhibitions you have. The way you interview staff. The brochures you write. Mark Twain said it well, 'If the patchwork is worth a $1,000, it's the stitches that make it work a million.' We did all of that for them; put the stitches in place and passionately debated what we thought was wrong). Six months later the chancellor called me. "Hello Aubrey, it's Bernard here, would you take our business back? The people we have now are not making it happen. Of course, if you say tough shit, I'll quite understand."

It wasn't that the new advisors were rubbish. They too had won many national and international awards for their marketing effectiveness. It was the fact that the strategy was being changed. And the fact that the new advisors lacked the time and patience to withstand the munch of the termites on their balls.

We took the business back. Bernard had big balls to go against the wishes of the termites!

Bernard was rare. But then, he was a maverick!

Now, how about one end of the spectrum to the other? From universities to the hot bed of pop. Yep, good pop groups are brands, usually established by a maverick. One day a guy who was a good friend of my brother's and who studied with my brother and me said, "I'm leaving the college." We asked him what he was going to do. "I'm going to be a pop star," he said, quietly and confidently. We sniggered a bit. (Particularly as he couldn't really sing well, or play an instrument that well either). A year later he was a pop star. A megapop star. He was the very queen of pop, Freddie Mercury.

Freddie had the vision, the idea of Queen. He picked the band members (he couldn't find a band that would have him!) He built the brand around him and decided how he would behave accordingly, forgive the pun, as 'brand leader!' He wrote most of the stuff with Brian May; they controlled the tone and style of the brand. The lessons? One objective - to become a pop star. To do that he did learn to sing and to play various instruments. He drove himself and the band. They focused and followed Freddie in everything they did, on and off stage.

When I tell you that Fred had a girlfriend, you can believe he was a maverick!

Want to hear about how the NFL exceeded their crowd estimates by over 28,000 in one game? In a country that didn't even understand American football? Well, that's another story...

## LESSONS LEARNT

• Focus on one vision.

• Don't have dreams, have goals (dream = 'imagined series of events, occurring during sleep', *Collins Dictionary*. Don't imagine it, do it!)

• You lead, and get like-minded followers around your vision, and get the others to get out of your way.

• One size does not fit all (have a close look at women's tights).

• If you don't have common sense, get someone in your team who does.

• Don't follow, blaze trails; original brand ideas come from original people.

• Question the past to make the future.

• Don't spend money on advertising, invest money in advertising and don't think advertising is the only way. Word of mouth, satisfied staff and customers are worth far more. Queen never really advertised; their performances were their advertisements!

• If you use staff recruitment advertising use it to advertise your brand as well as the job.

• Work with your external partners on your brand. If you have to treat them, or ever call them a 'supplier', then you don't have the right one. If they never argue with you or debate or question anything, and just do what you say, then you don't have the right one.

• As you grow don't have a committee, have a small number of expert advisors. You never see a statue to a committee.

• Hire the staff yourself. Do not just leave it up to HR.

• Be patient in growing your brand. It took us three years to get  one brand, Zam-Buk, moving and growing by 16%. Now it's grown by around 20%, over the past five years. It's now the biggest brand in our local client's portfolio.

• Brands last. Witness the tin below. I saw a member of staff using this little tin of Zam-Buk which she had been filling and refilling from the larger family-sized tin for many years. She even demanded this tin back after we photographed it, as she was so attached to it.

# UNDERMINING HONESTY

## HOW CAN YOU DIFFERENTIATE AND BUILD A TRUSTED BRAND?

Here's one way. How about the use of staggering honesty? Yep, the truth is that is what the customer wants. Give it to them and it'll work.

And it has already, in one of the most appealing advertising campaigns of the last century, in one of the most competitive markets in the world: real estate advertising in London. The estate agent, Roy Brooks, had a perfect insight into the potential buyer's mindset. Overstatement was, and still is, unfortunately common in advertising, and especially in the real estate market. Understatement is rare. By preparing the buyer for disaster, Brooks diminished the risk of high expectation being far greater than the actual experience. In fact, the buyers were often pleasantly surprised at what they found. Witness some of his cut-through-the-hyperbole copy opposite:

In other words, this advertised propperty can be refurbished and you could make a substantial profit...so hurry up and buy it.

**£5,995** **FHLD! Broken-down Batter-
sea Bargain.** Erected at end
of long reign of increasingly warped
moral & aesthetic values it's what you
expect—hideous; redeemed only by the
integrity of the plebs who built it—well.
Originally a one skiv Victorian lower-
middle class fmly res, it'll probably
be snapped up by one of the new Communications Élite, who'll tart it up &
flog it for 15 thou. 3 normal-sized
bedrms & a 4th for an undemanding
dwarf lodger, Bathrm. Big dble drawing
rm. B'fast rm & kit. Nature has fought
back in the gdn —& won. Call Sun 3-5
at 21 Surrey Lane, S.W.11. then Brooks.

**BETTER SORT OF TELY DIREC-
TOR** (Zoia & all that) & small
BLONDE ACTRESS'S FASH FUL-
HAM fmly res fabulous re-vamp
by famous Architects Stout &
Litchfield — thousands lavished.
Drawrm leading to dinrm, elegant,
comfortable, exciting, sliding wall
of glass to gdn of flowers, heavy
with scent of honeysuckle, Clema-
tis, runner beans, roses & love
apples, lawn secluded he says
" For natural sunbathing." A
Star's luxury kit, mod bathrm,
4 bedrms (3 DBLE) Big top one
ideal Studio/Study " Leaning out
of window o'er the trees music
softly wafts from Hurlingham &,
for a magic moment, the Class
barrier melts & you imagine yourself there amongst the nobs."
SACRIFICE £14,510 FHLD try
ANY offer. View Sun 736-1665
then Brooks.

So how did Brooks do? He became a household name in well-to- do property circles and amongst the property hunters of London. He became a brand. Brooks made an embarrassing fortune from his small ads. As a socialist he wasn't particularly comfortable with his wealth. So much so that he would load his Rolls Royce with shoes and deliver them to Russia.

CRICKETING PIANO MANUFACTURER MUST SELL FASHIONABLE ST. JOHN'S WD. modernised non-base. period house within earshot of Lords. 4 dble. bedrms., 2 bathrms.; Vanitory unit, cosy drawing rm., dining rm., kit./b'fast rm. CENT. HEAT MAGNIFICENT large 90ft. walled flower garden. big lawn or pitch, quite big enough for cricketer with soft ball to play on. GARAGE. LONG 80 yrs. Lse. G.R. £225 p.a. £15,750 try any offer. View Sun. CUN. 1681.

ONE OF THE FILTHIEST HOUSES I'VE SEEN FOR A LONG TIME. A crumbling corner period res. There are many things that can be said about FASHIONABLE PIMLICO: Dingy, for instance. 9 rms. (some quite fine altho' they've kept coal in a bedrm. & the drawing rm. chimney piece is sprawled across the flr.). Built in an age of elegance, contemporary I should think, with emperor LOUIS PHILLIPE, to restore it is about the only challenge left to a rich young couple today. ONLY £8,450. Lse. 80 yrs. G.R. ONLY £70. Keys Office.

He stood for honesty, and genuine straightforwardness. And no-one was immune from his sharp writing. When his friend, the British TV producer Desmond Wilcox, had his home up for sale, he had his bar in his sitting room described as, 'Rather theatrical and in keeping with the pretentious style of the owner.'

People went to the Roy Brooks ads. (Incidentally he used not one picture of the home for sale, ever. Just undermining honest copy.)

Hey, and another thing happened too. Sellers sought him out to sell their homes. In fact it was a sign of 'class' that Roy Brooks had his 'For Sale' sign outside your home!

I bet he had no problems with the call of many real estate agents of today, "I can't find enough stock, or I can't get my stock to sell!" No sirrr. He sold plenty, because he had a brand!

When Brooks died in 1971 his partners had published an anthology of the best of Brooks, "Brothel in Pamlico."

## BE HONEST: 'YOU'LL DIE'

This was the small advertisement that appeared in the London newspapers in 1900, written by the famous polar explorer, Ernest Shackleton.

The deadly frankness coupled with the simplicity probably made this the most cost-effective advertisement ever run. Shackleton said of the effect of the advertisement, "It seemed as though all the men in Great Britain were determined to accompany me, the response was so overwhelming."

(Many years later I had the honour of working, with Shackleton's great-grandson, Nick Shackleton, who had taken a leaf out of his great-grandfather's book. No, not as an explorer, but as an advertising copywriter. We worked on the Land Rover business...the nearest he got to exploring! Perhaps 50% of the talent was in the genes - the writing bit!)

I hope you will be inspired by some of the anecdotes and suggestions in this book. For me, the business has constantly taught me new things. And it still is.

MEN WANTED for Hazardous Journey. Small wages, bitter cold, long months of complete darkness, constant danger, safe return doubtful. Honor and recognition in case of success — Ernest Shackleton.

## WANTED

## 10 BRIGHT SPARKS

We're looking for 10 exceptional electricians to work in our team. If you're the brightest of sparks apply to
**Box No. G52648,**
**Selby Times, Southgate, Wakefield.**

## WANTED

## 10 PLUMBERS WHO HAVEN'T HAD A LEAK

We're looking for 10 top performing plumbers to work in our team. If you're hot apply to **Box No. G52648, Selby Times, Southgate, Wakefield.**

## WANTED

## 15 BRICKIES WHO WANT TO BUILD THEIR OWN LEGEND

We're looking for 15 exceptional bricklayers. You've got to be the best. Apply to **Box No. G52648, Selby Times, Southgate, Wakefield.**

Having read the Shackleton advertisement, and I never forgot it, it inspired us some time back to see if we could do the same for a building contractor! On the opposite page are some of the ads.

Did they work? Well, no and yes.

First of all, the client despite very strong pleas from us, would not let the ads run with their brand name. He just didn't think they would work (notice that we used a box number). Anxious to prove a point we, well I, actually, paid with the proviso that I be paid back five times the amount if they worked. Also, as the new artisans were required pronto we ran, at the client's insistence, an ordinary display recruitment advertisement.

So, what pulled? Ours did. Famously. In fact, the client called me over and said, "I can't believe it!" Pointing to a pile of papers on his desk he added, "Look, I've never seen the likes of this before, plumbers and electricians have actually written curriculam vitae!"

They found the staff they wanted. Top-notch too. We wrote simple challenging ads, and winners replied.

Two anecdotes to that. The project they recruited those brickies, sparks, and plumbers for was built, on time and on budget and the contractor received no penalties…And the other? Well, you can't win them all. We did have one brickie who phoned in and said he wanted to know where 'Leg-End' (legend) was, as he couldn't find it on the map, and he wanted to see if he could travel there easily from home!

# THE VALUE OF BEING SMALL

In the world of brands, is big, always beautiful?

Not always. As self-actualisation and the need to be an 'individual' motivates men and women's behaviour, small brands can become increasingly attractive. And by 'small' I mean, either in reality, or perceptually.

'Small' can positively mean exclusive, hand-made or carefully put together, while conversely, 'big' can mean for everyone, mass-produced and quickly put together.

Attach those attributes to a beer. Which one would you prefer to drink: one from a small brewery, or one from a large one? Maybe it's the beer from the smaller brewery? In urban South Africa out of the top ten beers 'regularly drunk' 40% are beers perceptually considered to be small. Consumers are getting selective. Small is good.

Jack Daniel's is an example of how 'small' makes you big. Jack Daniel's tone and manner, the way they present themselves, reeks of the values of a small Lynchburg distillery stuck in the past, where whittling a stick is part of the distiller's art, to pass the time-of-day, as the wort gently changes to alcohol. The distillery is, unlike a lot of America, unhindered by progress!

Compare that with a distillery in Scotland, Glengoyne, which produces a whisky so deliciously silky and smooth that 'it goes down singing hymns'. Their positive brand baggage was that they were small. Very small. I seem to remember that no more than eight people worked there. Water tumbled down from the Campsie Fells (the hillside that overlooked the distillery) and curled and swirled into the wee loch above the distillery, where it rested a while before being 'invited' into the distillery. There it would infuse with the malted barley in a glorious haze of steam and produce an aroma like the sweet smell of freshly mown straw with a mere whiff of demarara - enough to clear the chest of severely blocked bronchial tubes. Hallelujah!

## BEWARE OF ACCOUNTANTS

We persuaded the marketing director and his team to run a series of small advertisements tucked away in newspapers. Offering directions, via the winding roads, to the distillery, as 'the train no longer traveled into the hills'. We told about the 'tunnel and hidden pipeline under the small road' that passed the distillery gates, 'so the whisky could go under the road, and into the barrels',

**WE HAVE JUST FOUND** a quote from the "World Guide to Whisky" where the author said good things about our GLENGOYNE 10 YEAR OLD SINGLE HIGHLAND MALT so we have clubbed together to tell you what he said ‗ in his £14.95 fine book. He said,  "it is steadily gaining in admirers" and mentioned, "it has a light to medium body with a rounded fruitiness" . . . we are, "not famous but are gaining admirers". Quite frankly the few of us couldn't produce a lot if we were famous. Our distillery is very small and quite cramped and since 1833 has been distilling Glengoyne very well. Locally people say, "it goes down singing hymns". And that is praise enough. Thank you.

## THE GLENGOYNE DISTILLERY

Glengoyne. Scotland. Telephone 254.

**WE ARE PLEASED TO ANNOUNCE** after placing only 4 adverts in this newspaper our GLENGOYNE 10 YEAR OLD SINGLE HIGHLAND MALT is steadily gaining awareness. Sales are doing very well. However, ac‑ cording to our stillman he thinks our  modest success has something to do with the fact that the recipe hasn't changed for the past 150 years and a recent Sunday Telegraph survey 'An Expert Guide to Scotland's Finest Malt Whiskies' said very good things about our taste. It said we have "a sweet honeyed character". Our mashman agrees with our stillman. He thinks advertising is a waste of money. Anyway whatever the reason for our continued success, after 150 years of effort, it's nice to know we're doing so well. Thank you for supporting us.

## THE GLENGOYNE DISTILLERY

Glengoyne. Scotland. Telephone 254.

avoiding the need to stop the odd car and local family of ducks that 'happened by'. We even offered free samples of the Glengoyne Malt Whisky miniatures by post. Another advertisement apologised for the fact that we couldn't supply enough whisky, as the distillery was geographically hemmed in by the hills on one side and the road on the other. And anyway, even if we could expand to meet the growing demand, we wouldn't, because producing Glengoyne this old, time-honoured and limited way was the only way. Only the avaricious with an insatiable appetite for profit would expand. We were distillers.

Another advertisement sang the praises of Michael Jackson (no, not the *Thriller*, moon dancing character, but the Michael Jackson who wrote *The World Guide to Whisky*) who said Glengoyne 'Was steadily gaining admirers,' and it was, for sales were up and many of us were happy with our wee campaign. Except one: the chairman of the distillery. He wanted to be chairman of a big distillery, and emotionally one can understand that, and Glengoyne was becoming big but perceptually remained small. That was its success.

And that is Jack Daniel's success. If you go to Lynchburg, go to the distillery. Or, visit their web site. They have become a huge success and the distillery and the surrounding buildings take up a fair few acres, but perceptually they remain small. And by the way they do whittle sticks. The most action they see in a day is the changing of a light bulb. And they are true to all their advertisements, particularly to the one that featured the distinctive square bottle, and said something like, 'The accountant said make the bottle round, the distiller said keep it square. Who remembers the name of the accountant!'

Beware of accountants.

## SO, YOU WANT TO STAY SMALL TO BE BIG?

Being small doesn't always work. When the advertising agency Rightford Searle-Tripp and Makin was small, in the 1980s, they were very successful, because they also acted big. They had a very powerful presentation that showed their depth of understanding of the South African market and their links with Stellenbosch University. They published a regular Indaba newssheet that debated trends. Their passion was big. And their leader, Bob Rightford, not that tall, was a giant to work with. A big personality. So although small from a staffing point of view, they were big in performance and positioning. They picked up all the awards and the best staff too. So make sure, before you think you want to remain 'small', that that is right for the well-being of your company or brand.

Here's a checklist that we put together for the brewery that we grew from 45th in the market to 4th in the market in the UK.

We wanted to be perceived as:

• Not available everywhere

- For the discerning drinker ✓

- Having an interesting range of beers ✓

- Being made the same way for years ✓

- Real Yorkshire beer ✓

This brand imagery test gave us scores in the 85 to 95% range.

Conversely, we did not want to be perceived as:

- High-tech ✗

- Modern ✗

- Available everywhere ✗

Advertisement descriptors, the language the respondents used to describe the advertisements, were rated in the 70 to 98% range for:

- Believable ✓

- Informative ✓

- Good impression ✓

- Interesting ✓

- Convincing ✓

# OTHER WAYS OF GETTING NOTICED

In 1909 the first singing commercial for Castle was staged. The scene was the old Empire Palace of Variety in Jo'burg. On stage was a comedian, wearing a preposterous hat, who broke into a song entitled, 'The drink of the day', with words by a guy called Foster and music by Montagu. Some of the lyrics went thus:

> 'So I called on a friend of brewery fame,
>
> It's the best that I know, called Castle by name...
>
> For all other stouts now I don't care a jot,
>
> Castle's own oatmeal's the best of the lot'

This song was greeted so enthusiastically that *The Sunday Times*, the first and last time in its history, devoted one whole page of free editorial to the words and music. By today's standards that would mean around R370,000 worth of free advertising and as it was seen as PR that would be worth around six times that amount. A whopping R2,200,000.

Previously, in 1904, Castle had also taken centre stage, as the world's strongest man, George Hackneyschmidt (who had been invited to South Africa by South African Breweries), raised a barrel of Castle above his head, amongst various muscular marvels,

resulting in thousands of publicity photographs being distributed and calendars being published and Castle memorabilia being manufactured and sold.

Today advertising agencies, clients and promotional companies talk of 360° Communications, Brand Activation Programmes and Integrated Programmes, focusing on the need to interrupt and engage the consumer in different and unexpected ways. Really, as the old line for Castle said, 'Nothing's changed'. It's only the circumstances that have changed. The environment and context that the industry works in is driving us to think differently, just as it did then. Then, there was no TV, or radio or cinema. So the 'creatives', whoever they were in the early 1900s - perhaps it was Castle's founders and the two partners of Charles Glass? Pioneers Jim Walsh, a coach operator working between Ladysmith and Barberton, and H.B. Marshall, who both financed Charles Glass's Castle brewery in Marshall's township in Jo'burg, and later bought Charles Glass out. After all, they were, as early pioneers, entrepreneurial thinkers, knew no boundaries, and had a good eye for an opportunity - as any decent 'creative' should, no matter which era they are from.

Today we have even more media clutter to attend to than those early pioneers had. Now there is a barrage of TV, radio, cinema, outdoor, wap, warp, MMS, internet, Facebook.

*Fortissimo*

# STAND UP AND SING

So perhaps we should turn backwards to go forwards? Why not a man in a funny hat standing up and singing the praises of Castle lager? Better still, a praise singer who stands up in the middle of a London or New York cinema, and extols the virtues of a holiday in South Africa; or stands in the middle of Central Park, New York, and gives praise to the wonders of a South African holiday…That would get a few lines in *The New York Times*, an interview on radio and TV… That would break through the cacophony of media clutter in the good old US of A!

*The impossible pub that moved in Britain and in the USA.*

## AFTER A FEW PINTS THE PUB BEGINS TO MOVE?

Or to promote a range of beers, why not a beer tent? Or better still, build a full-size pub - one that can travel around the countryside and sell ale; complete with oak-panelled walls, beams, solid wooden floor, traditional pub furniture, historical artifacts and a beer garden outside. Impossible?

Not at all. Such a thing was conceived and built for brewers T&R Theakston in England. Complete with a temperature-controlled mobile 'cellar' mounted in a 17.5-ton truck, a team of riggers, drivers, bar staff and managers, it toured the shows and pop concerts in the UK and even went to the USA, dispensing Theakston Traditional Ales. The bar was 64 feet long and could serve up to 1,500 pints of beer an hour - 18,000 pints a day.

Perhaps the most remarkable thing was it looked absolutely real and very old, matching the brand values of Theakston Ales. So convincing was it that an official survey of the area where it was being built and first assembled marked the Black Bull Inn as a permanent building and local pub! You can imagine the surprise when this treasured landmark disappeared overnight,

The advertisement for the "Pub That Moved". In three days at one event the pub had 15 000 visitors and wherever it went, it created news far exceeding the advertising expenditure, as can be seen at the bottom of the opposite page.

headed down the motorway (in one 44-foot truck, accompanied by the 40-foot support vehicle and 17.5-ton mobile 'cellar') and appeared in the South West of England three days later. Perhaps this was the event that inspired the copywriter from the advertising agency that had the account and was promoting the pub to write the enticing headline, under a picture of the Black Bull Inn, 'After a few pints of Theakston, the pub begins to move.'

The point of this case-history is that it illustrates several aspects of modern communications. The idea was born out of a thorough understanding of the brand and the appeal to the consumer. It was quirky and very traditional. Its appeal was, paradoxically, that it was not available everywhere and the strategy was, one of 'Now you see us, now you don't,' to whet the appetite and give the ale its scarce and hard-to-come-by persona. The marketing director put it another way: 'If Mohammed (the consumer) can't come to the mountain (our brewery and attached pub) then the mountain will go to Mohammed.'

*Good P.R creates free advertising and is worth a small fortune.*

The 'creatives' who conceived the idea were the same team who conceived all of the Theakston work - advertising, promotions, direct marketing, trade relations, and  even the design of the Visitor's Centre at the 'real' brewery and pub in North Yorkshire, England. There was one conductor of the 'orchestra' and a team (with the client), who had a shared vision, and had written a very succinct brand print to guide, inspire, and brief all communications work, regardless of discipline. Too often these days, the brand 'orchestra' plays out of tune, without a single conductor. The promotional company can pull the tone of the brand in one direction, a direct marketing company call pull it in another, and so on. The result? No coherent brand, and worse still, the client's marketing budget dissipates. A brand should be 'dressed in one consistent suit of clothes'.

Advertising agencies are addressing this problem and offering a 'one conductor' scenario. However, some 'creatives' who produce the brand advertising are so egotistical that they, 'Don't do promotions,' (preferring the glamour of making TV commercials instead) and certainly, 'don't do junk mail' (that's direct mail, or Customer Relationship Marketing, and the only reason it was ever called 'junk' was because in some quarters it was being handled by below-par 'creatives'). If you want to see some great direct marketing get onto the Peterman Catalogue:

www.jpeterman.com

## The J Peterman Coat

"Classic Horseman's duster protects you, your rump, your saddle and legs down to your ankles. Because it's very long to do the job, it's unintentionally very flattering. With, or without a horse!"

J. Peterman

## WATCH OUT FOR IN-FIGHTING

The other problem is that advertising agencies, like any sensible business, need to keep afloat, so they need to chase the bucks. And more of the bucks have been going away from advertising (now only 25% of some clients' budgets) and into below-the-line (now often 75%). In chasing the bucks they offer the below-the-line services and, to do that they have many departments, and many heads of departments, all of which have their own financial targets and this creates silos, which creates competition and in-fighting. Clients aren't shared, but jealously guarded and consequently clients don't always get what is right for them, but what is right for the bottom line of a particular department head who, 'Needs to make budget'.

Robyn Putter, formaly creative head of WPP, asked me to put forward a proposal on how to solve this within Ogilvy, and I remember him nodding in agreement with the 16-page presentation, proposal and arguments that I had put together, along with my recommendation to 'test market' a unit within Ogilvy, with one open-minded, business-orientated, experienced creative head conducting it, with specialists under him, or her. Robyn nodded, then shook his head, "How can we do this, when 'Brian' (not the real name of the the very senior creative director Robyn referred to) doesn't even understand what you and I are talking about?"

Since that discussion, I believe headway has been made.

## HOW TO AVOID, 'HEY, I AM A COMMERCIAL MESSAGE, PLEASE IGNORE ME!'

The other lesson is the value of PR. Again, too often spurned by the advertising agency and often, in tit-for-tat, the advertising agency is despised by PR. Yet the value of PR is enormous, especially in a marketplace where the consumer is often cynical towards advertising messages (as research in this country is already indicating). In fact, PR is valued in space, or time terms, six times as much as the equivalent space or time used for an advertising message. Why? Because PR doesn't carry with it the label of 'I am a commercial message, please read me'. So, it gets through the clutter of advertising. Remember, consumers watch TV for the programmes, read magazines for the articles, listen to the radio for news and the programmes and so forth - not to see the advertisements our industry slaves over. Sounds pretty obvious? I think so, but a client of mine once gaily announced that his target audience actually bought magazines to read the advertisements! I wish.

So PR gets through the clutter. The secret is to make sure that the PR people understand the brand and its values and don't think that column centimetres in an obscure magazine, that your target never reads are of any value at all. Neither should they think that a national daily is of any use if the target audience doesn't read that too. Start with the strategy, what you need to say to whom, and then use media research to draw up a list of publications and media. Target them and make sure what is going out and what is published or flighted carries the values of the brand. Too often PR does not receive the planning, and careful writing and nurturing it deserves. Being a good writer does not automatically make you good for PR. You must understand strategy and brands, first.

## DO THE IMPOSSIBLE

You can do the impossible. The Black Bull Inn, the travelling pub we spoke about earlier, was a big idea. The cynics said 'impossible'. It made a lot of people snigger and a lot of people very nervous. Nervous is good. We didn't sleep at night. Every day we remembered the idea and discussed it. Every nail, screw, bolt, chair, table, light, picture, and piece of wallpaper and floorboard was worried about. Because everyone was discussing it, and getting very excited, and nervous, we knew we had a team that was focused and that cared. We fussed about it as much as agency writers and art directors fuss about their ads...Hell, this *was* an ad! A bloody great ad! And if it was built properly it was going to make big news. And it did. "Pub that travels as well as its ale," said one paper; "Britain's only Travelling Pub," said another, and there were local TV and radio interviews. It created millions of pounds' worth of advertising. In three days at one event it had 15,000 visitors. It created 15,000 Theakston pilgrims, as we called them, and nearly all of them bought a promotional item, each created in line with the brand personality, like a watch that went backwards in time, a set of humanoid dice, a set of spoofing coins, a pen made out of brass and oak from a Theakston barrel that retailed at over R600 and playing cards (that are now collectors' items). And in turn, almost every visitor's details went onto our database and they received up-dates on the Black Bull Inn's next appearance, when the range of Theakston Draught Ales would be available in their local pub and when the bottled ales would be available in the local supermarket.

*This limited edition fountain pen was hand-crafted from one of the Theakston oak casks. Handsome and heavy it writes like a dream. For sale at the travelling pub, it helped gather a database of Theakston drinkers. The pen became a top-seller and is still writing the records books today.*

The hard sales data? As part of an ongoing programme, the brand output increased by

# 542%.

On an emotional level it received two top Advertising Effectiveness Awards (one in the UK and one in the USA) and a hatful of Creative Awards (for Advertising, Design, Customer Relationship Marketing, Promotions and a Film Documentary).

# CAN PEOPLE
# BECOME BRANDS?

CAN PEOPLE BECOME BRANDS?

## CAN PEOPLE BECOME BRANDS?

You bet they can. And they already have. Here are some: Chanel, Ford, Pierre Cardin (a director friend of mine overheard a guy in the Free State ask for a tracksuit made by him, except that he said 'Hey man, haven't you got a tracksuit made by Perry Cardigan?').

My big boss David Ogilvy was one. In fact, Ogilvy & Mather was once known simply as, 'Ogilvy', using a derivative of David's signature as the company logo.

Long before the industry was talking about making brands David was doing it for himself and for his string of advertising agencies around the globe.

He laid down the 'DNA' through what he called, his 'Magic Lantern' presentations - a series of slide presentations on the 'rules' (the brand personality) of what Ogilvy believed made advertising work and sell. When no other agency had any 'rules', David had loads. The staff knew them; clients knew them and came to Ogilvy because they believed in them. They believed in the David Ogilvy way of doing things, the Ogilvy brand and what the brand offered. In short, when the industry had little professionalism, few theories, or guidelines, Ogilvy had them.

avid Ogilvy - founder of the Ogilvy empire. He became the industry leader, the guru, and s agency became the brand leader.

I guess these days you would call them, something like 'vision, mission and purpose'. Somehow we like to hang tags on everything, mostly meaningless, full of ambiguity, and certainly misunderstood too.

Here though are some meaningful ones, about Ogilvy people, written by David:

• You can divide advertising people into two groups-the amateurs and the professionals. The amateurs are the majority. They aren't students of advertising. They guess. The professionals don't guess, so they don't waste so much of their clients' money.

• The most important function in advertising is the creative function. But only one in 10 of the people in agencies work in the creative department. The account executives outnumber the copywriters two to one. If you owned a dairy farm, would you employ twice as many milkers as cows?

• You can't bore people into buying your product, you can only interest them in buying it.

• The most important ingredient in any agency is the ability of the top man to lead his troops.

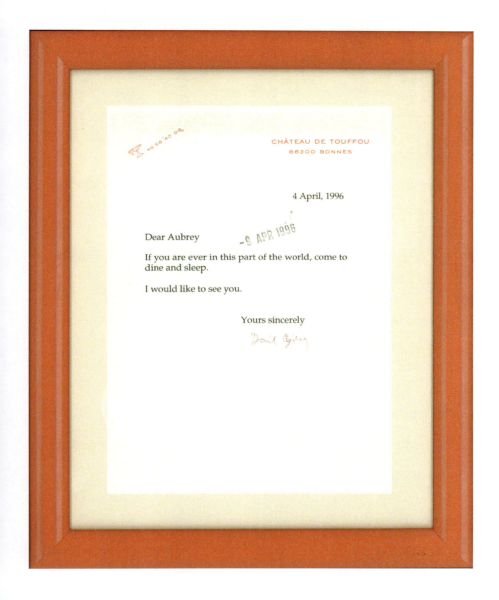

CHÂTEAU DE TOUFFOU
86300 BONNES

4 April, 1996

Dear Aubrey          -9 APR 1996

If you are ever in this part of the world, come to dine and sleep.

I would like to see you.

Yours sincerely

*First David Ogilvy fires me and then he invites me to dinner!*

He wrote books, imparting his knowledge and experience. He gave lectures and talks. He became the industry leader. The guru. The brand leader.

And David led from the top. The image, equity, knowledge and behaviour of David and his agencies was the same, no matter where you went, from London, New York, Paris, Thailand or South Africa. We all wore, 'The same suit of clothes'.

I think David was the first to wear red braces. So the offices reflected them by having red carpets. And the staff wore T-shirts with red braces printed on them. The 'Magic Lanterns' were published all over the world as a series of 'How to...' ads. The same ads hung in the corridors, with red frames. The stationery, publications, and sign were red. Videos of the 'Magic Lantern' presentations were made and distributed as business tools.

David dressed the same way (yep, the same suit of clothes), wherever he went; three piece tweed suit, pipe and braces. And as a Scot with short arms and deep pockets, he rarely paid for lunch and nearly always smoked someone else's tobacco!

# CAN PEOPLE BECOME BRANDS?

CHÂTEAU DE TOUFFOU
86300 BONNES
FRANCE

February 26, 1992

Dear Patrick

I congratulate you on organizing hikes and backpacking trails.

As for my designing a T-shirt, forget it. I abominate them, and throw away the half-dozen or so which are sent to me every year.

A shirt with writing on it is the last word in bad taste. Or so I think.

\* \* \* \*

Yours

David Ogilvy

(Typed in Paris)

*David Ogilvy had very fixed opinions and detested the idea of T-shirts carrying brand and product messages. Witness the T-shirt to the right, produced by Ogilvy Jo'burg after Patrick Shamley of Ogilvy Jo'burg wrote to David!*

## BE RUTHLESS: FIRE THE BRAND TRANSGRESSORS

He had his rules and he was pretty ruthless in making sure we adhered to them. Rules about type. Rules about how the headline should be under the picture. Rules about subheads and long copy in advertising. I should know how strict he was about these rules, for I broke one of them by suggesting and then negotiating to use Sir Paul McCartney to compose a track for one of the WWF films we were about to make. He had me removed. (Although some years later he eased up a bit and said, 'Rules are for fools, but for the guidance of wise men'. And he invited me for dinner at his Chateau in Touffou, France).

## THE CHAIRMAN IS THE BRAND CONDUCTOR

The lesson here was that David was the brand. The custodian, the owner and rightly, the guardian. He stood for order, knowledge and intelligence, gathered over many years of producing advertising that worked. His character and behaviour was inseparable from that of the Ogilvy & Mather Agencies. And clients bought that. They bought him. I was fired because I broke one of the rules of the brand by suggesting we use a pop star to promote a serious organisation. Although I tried to enlist the support of Ogilvy people and WWF people in Geneva, where WWF's HQ was, the reply was the same: "Aubrey, you are right in what you have proposed but you have opened up a can of worms with David; he simply does not believe that a pop star is right for a serious organisation like WWF, but it's OK for chewing gum!"

## WHY SIR RICHARD BRANSON'S BRANDS FLY

We've spoken about Sir Richard Branson being a brand. Like Ogilvy his values are his company's values, the Virgin values. If Sir Richard were to leave Virgin for another organisation, Virgin would change. If Sir Richard were to buy, let's say, Land Rover, the values of Land Rover would change. The cars would be like no other. If he bought one of our big banks, imagine the change!

Whatever he does, he doesn't follow the established rules. With his Virgin Atlantic airline he broke the rules: he has masseurs on board the aircraft, and a poolside lounge, office and library, cocktail bar, even a Cowshed spa and Bumble hairdresser in their executive lounge in Heathrow. He has Economy and Premium Economy (same food, more leg-room); no First Class or Business Class, but Upper Class! His magazine is not some bumptious publication but is simply called 'Hot Air!' Sir Richard Branson's entrepreneurial attitude and 'helpful' values permeate and drive all his businesses. When I flew from London to Australia via LA, during the Gulf War, with a serious back injury and a special support for my back, the Virgin Atlantic check-in staff spotted me and said, "One moment please." Seconds later they had up-graded me and my wife to Upper Class. I was literally relieved. The flight, which was going to be painful, was now a joy.

Here's some of Sir Richard's advice from his book, *Screw it, Let's do it*

• Make a difference, help others.

• Always think, what can you do to help.

• Believe it can be done.

I always fly Virgin Atlantic, when I can.

'A brand is a product dressed in a relevant and consistent suit of clothes.' This was the definition we used earlier in this book. It's interesting to note that Sir Richard Branson has always looked more or less the same. And has dressed the same: the impish smile and toothy grin accompanied by a jumper and open-necked shirt. Relaxed. Easy-going. Like Virgin Atlantic. Like his brand.

David Ogilvy, three piece suit, tie and pipe. Studious, knowledgeable, like his brand.

## STARS ARE BRANDS AND THEY MAKE MORE  s

Pop stars are brands. Freddie Mercury is one example. Freddie was Queen. When Freddie died, Queen, the band, died.

Some, very successful movie stars are brands. Their instant 'brand code' tells the filmgoer what to expect. They are guaranteed a certain kind of movie experience.

Bruce Willis = action. Hugh Grant = Englishman in romantic comedy. Julia Roberts = romance. Sylvester Stallone = muscle-bound action hero.

Julia Roberts has become the highest-paid actress in the world, topping *Hollywood Reporter's* top-earning female stars for four consecutive years (2002-2005). She was paid an unprecedented $25 million for her role in *Mona Lisa Smile*. Her net worth is estimated to be $140 million. Her films have grossed $2 204 631 930 at the American box office, making her the biggest movie star in history - reaching the feat with only 31 films.

Although Stallone has been indentified and positioned as specialising in playing incoherent muscle men, he is no dummy. His screenplay for Rocky was an Oscar nomination. But he knows his value as a strong single-minded recognisable brand. "I've been identified with a certain kind of physicality and so for me to expect to be Daniel Day-Lewis would be futile. It took me many years to figure out that you can't do everything. You got specialilities...". Stallone, who turned down $5 million in 1988 for an appearance in a beer commercial, refusing to cut his hair (changing the brand?) also said, "I am a manifestation of my own fantasy." A manifestation that receives around $20 million a picture and at the age of 61 was making yet another muscular appearance as John Rambo.

Bruce Willis earned $100 million - the highest earnings for any actor, at the time of being in the 1999 movie *The Sixth Sense*. Movies that have featured him, or had him playing a supporting role, have grossed between $2.55 billion to $3.04 billion!

Some actors avoid being stereotyped, and usually make a little less money too.

*Stallone turned down millions for an appearance in a beer commercial refusing to cut his hair - changing the brand?*

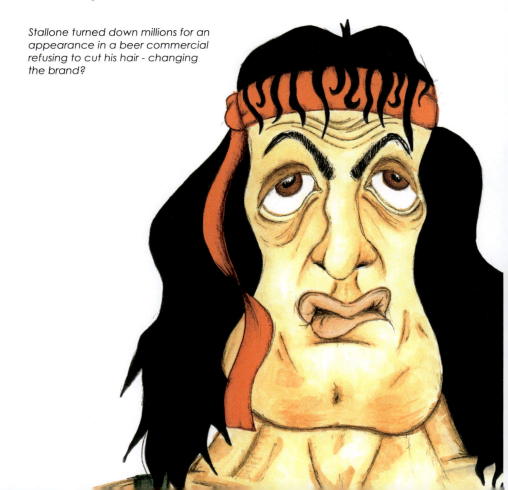

# WEB SITES.
# DON'T MAKE YOUR
# TARGET AUDIENCE
# WAIT.

So you want to embark on designing and building, or refreshing your own website? Well, here goes...

It's not any easy task. All you have to do is browse a few sites and see how much rubbish is out there. Millions of bucks spent on sites that the moment a customer clicks on the site they click off. With Internet usage growing this job is only worth doing well. The commercial ramifications of doing it well are enormously satisfying.

Witness the reworking of a website we did for a small Boutique Hotel which had a miserable occupancy rate of around 12%. We completely redesigned the site, rewrote the copy, took new photographs and badgered the client into doing it properly including a lot of work and considerable expertise in the area of Search Engine Optimisation, which we worked closely with an expert on. Now their occupancy rate is up to 98%.

There are some basic rules about designing a site that will work hard for you and pay back in "clicks!" And "clicks" mean more customers! All the basic rules relate to speed and easy access.

First design it and execute in such a way that who ever clicks on your site gets instant gratification, immediate access to your website. No spinning time wheels no slow downloading pictures, or silly frustrating scrolling time lines. One click and the customer should be into your site. If they are kept waiting, as I have often done (and I'm sure you have too) your customer will be off and onto a competitor's site. And you'll have a lost sale or enquiry. And they'll never come back for a frustrating and time consuming experience again.

Next, the "Don't make me think." This is often known as "The rule of usability, or simplicity."

What it means is that once a customer gets onto your site it must be self-evident the way they should navigate around the site. No scratching of heads or wondering what it means if they would click on that button or another.

Some of the culprits are over designed sites, where you just don't know where to look, there's no formality in the design, no clear visual hierarchy on what to look at first. Not easy to look at and "take-in" the layout must be simple for the brain and eye "to catch.". I liken this to when someone chucks a dozen tennis balls in the air for you to catch, you can't catch them all, and indeed you probably become so confused you drop the lot!

Other problems include using bad taglines on your homepage. These meaningless taglines are usually some internal mission statement incomprehensible by your customer. If you have a bad one, don't use it, or rewrite it. The best I've seen is for a hi-fi company, "We thrill people with sound." They tell it like it is, it engages and delivers. Not surprisingly they are world leaders in Hi-Fi equipment.

So, if you are to use a tag line make sure it unambiguously reflects your offer, loud and clear.

Other culprits include unfamiliar naming of the tabs, cute and clever names or names that have been thought up by marketing people or unfamiliar industry names. "Products" is better than

*How many tennis balls can you see?*
*And how many can you actually catch?*

"Product Lines." "Product Demarcations" even worse. " Jobs" is better than "Hirings." If your customer has to stop and think and try and interpret what the tab means…they will be off the site in a second. Every question they have to ask themselves, "What does this tab/word mean, how should I interpret that?" increases their frustration with the site and you, the company. And people don't do business with a company who you have to "wait" to be served or don't like because of the way they don't "connect" with you.

The home page should be clear what you do and who you are. It must convey the big picture. It should be able to answer four questions in the customer's head, "What do they have here for me?" "What can I do on this site?" Why should I stay on this site and not go anywhere else?" "Will I be able to navigate this site quickly and easily, or will it frustrate me?"

With the visual hierarchy make sure you obey the rules. On each page make sure you understand and represent what is more important than the next thing. It sounds so obvious; use size of type to distinguish what is most important

**(BOLD type and a larger size)** than what is least important (normal weight type and smaller).

Writing copy for a website is hard and it's different. Never think of your website as a catalogue. It isn't. The copy needs to engage, entice and delight. Use subheads to draw the customer's attention to a certain feature or a benefit. Use question marks to suck the reader in.

**WANT TO KNOW WHAT IS ON THE NEXT PAGE?**

See?
They suck
you in.

*What's going on here? Question marks in your advertising copy
will suck the reader in.*

Use the "Walk Test" to see how to construct your site. Sketch it out on a wipe board. Imagine you are walking into a store and you are at the ground floor entrance (the home page). What does this store offer and where can I find it? Ok, right, now I have to click onto that tab, "Products" to go and find it. This is it; I want the electrical department because I'm looking for a light fitting. So now I arrive at the electrical department and I click on light fittings and hey presto that's the one I want. There's a picture of it, the measurements, the technical spec and all the prices. Now where to pay? Ah there it is, "Check Out" or perhaps I need to go to "Sales Enquiries" as I want to see if they have it in brass...

So, within about 6 clicks I got what I wanted. I didn't have to wait and I didn't have to interpret what each tab or drop down meant. East peesy as it should be.

A final few words. One you have the site-up and running (and before you go public) get a few people who don't know your business to navigate their way round the site. Try some "Usability Tests" and see how easy and quick it is to use and make the modifications necessary.

# IT'S THE SOCIAL MEDIA PHENOMENON - SO SOCIALISE!

This burgeoning and ever-changing series of "platforms" is flourishing and mutating everyday.

For that reason I do not wish to dwell on it for too long and in particular the "platforms". As one thing is for sure, as soon as the ink is dry on this page there will be another "platform" that's appeared and a rush to explore it and use it commercially and privately.

So, as to make sure you get value for money from visiting these few pages in this book I will point out a few basic rules to help guide you in your decision to, or not to, fraternize with and benefit from being within this wonderful social media world.

Used and invested in properly social media platforms, like Facebook, Twitter, LinkedIn, Google Plus AND even YouTube are very adept at creating communities in which like-minded people can use and above all, enjoy. You are creating a conversation, a liaison, and hopefully a genuine friendship with like-minded people. And above all you can be rewarded with a loyal and growing customer base.

*Friends make friends.*

Even using these platforms for personal reasons is very similar (although some may not agree) to the way you should use them for business reasons. As an individual you will have certain values you uphold and live by, and that is exactly the same as in business. We call them brand values. And brand values can, and should be adhered to if you want to build relationships. Either your own brand (which incidentally you can build see pages 171 to 183) and of course, your business brand.

So before you embark on any social media usage for your brand make sure you have a set of values that reflect how you want your company to be seen and what's more important, a set of values that are relevant, appealing and engaging for your customers and potential customers. Be objective when you write them down. Ask yourself are these values relevant to my target audience? Or do they just make you feel warm and cuddly towards your own brand. As I believe Lyndon Johnson (36th President of the USA) said, "It's a bit like pissing down your own leg, it may seem hot to you, but it never does anything for anyone else."

Once you have these values down on paper, gauge everything you do against the list.

These platforms are called "Social" for good reason because they are used to "Socialise" with (hopefully) like-minded people. So the over-riding principle is make sure that your tone, manner and style is social. That is very often a very different tone to that you would use in many other forms of communication and advertising. Social language should be friendly, very chatty and of interest to the person you are "talking" to and "discussing" issues with. Many companies have made the mistake of bragging on social media. Brag and you will get a healthy 2 fingers from your followers.

*Brag and it's thumbs down.*

Don't make the mistake of thinking that social media platforms are a replacement for advertising. If you are making offers be careful how you do that. No CAPITAL letters. For example whilst billboards and TV create awareness and have impact, social media should be there to have a conversation about your brand. Whilst print and radio deliver messages, they have no interaction with the consumer. Social media allows you to "woo" your customers. And because it's interactive, between "you and them" it allows you to build a strong bond with your customers. To understand their needs and desires. And to win them over and perhaps motivate them to talk about your brand and share its values (both emotional and rational) with others.

Do not hide behind anonymity. Use your real name in posts and tweets. Fake names, or no names means you must have a reason to hide. Can your new, or potential "friend" trust someone who hides? You'll notice on many web sites ( another social platform) these days, under "contacts" there are no names, just a contact form. There are often  no email addresses. No physical address. No telephone numbers. Many of these sites are governmental… not surprisingly! But now, many are brand companies. Doesn't that annoy you? Doesn't that make you feel uneasy? You don't make friends with someone who doesn't give you their name! You move onto someone who does.

Hello my name is
## JOE BLOGS

Keep the site live. If you toss your hat into the social media ring make sure you have the commitment, the time and budget to keep up-dating the site with useful information. Be committed to reply to those that make contact. Be committed to create and supply "New News" to your followers. No "New News" no interaction means you are "so last week," disrespectful…maybe even, just, "gone-away."

**Be prepared to: -**

1. Share information several times a day.

2. Respond to comments and enquiries quickly (apparently a piece of research shows that those that Tweet expect a reply in 60 minutes)!

3. Provide information, indeed, be entertaining before even attempting to sell.

4. Welcome new friends.

5. Don't talk about the "Company" (that's cold and unfriendly) use " we" and and "us."

6. Absolutely do not try and inflate your own balloon by "Liking" you own post, or asking for "Likes," "Comments," and "Shares." That's a bit like sending yourself a Valentine's Card. Once discovered, it's a bit sad, isn't it?

SO YOU THINK
YOU MIGHT WANT TO
PRODUCE YOUR OWN
ADVERTISING?

## DO YOU, OR DON'T YOU?

Many clients, big and small have a desire to want to produce their own advertising, circumventing the advertising professionals and therefore saving money. Allegedly.

My advice is don't. I wouldn't want to remove my own (vermiform) appendix myself, I am not a trained doctor and would not only be squeamish at the thought, I would be inept at the procedure and would undoubtedly kill myself along the way.

So, if you decide to "Do it Yourself" you may not end-up killing yourself, but you could end-up killing your business and taking valuable time that would be better used in doing what you are good at and trained for.

However, there are some examples of small businesses that have taken on their own mantel of becoming their own advertising agency and have succeeded. Some quite handsomely. So over the next few pages I am going to be sharing with you some logical steps (that I have learnt over my 30+ years making bucks for clients) along with a few examples of how some companies have done it themselves, and done very well out of it as well.

But the single lesson to be learnt, to begin with, you have to start-out with a product that people want. Not a product you just want to sell.

How many times do you see, as I see in the city where I live, little shops opening and closing because the owner says they want to sell jewellery. Or they like the glamorous idea of opening and running a cocktail bar. Or a hardware store, when a few kilometers away there are 3, yes 3 massive hardware stores.

So it's not what you would like to do, it's what people would like to buy that's important. And if you have something you like doing, or making and people want it, then that's Utopia, isn't it? And Utopia is a perfect and rewarding state to be in.

So if you think you have an original business, with a service or product, or products that have clear benefits and that could clearly differentiate you from others I'll meet you in the next few pages and we'll begin to sell your dream, your Utopia…

If you don't have an appetite, and feel a little

*Ouch. Are you sure you want to do it yourself?*

squeamish about taking the step to doing it yourself, call in the professionals. Hints on how to find them are on pages 97 to 113 of this book.

## BEFORE YOU ADVERTISE, THINK.

The natural thing to do, when you want to create some advertising is to rush ahead and create it.

My advice is don't, not quite yet.

Going ahead and advertising without some fundamental research is like going into battle with out any reconnaissance. The Brits did that during the Boer war and failed, especially at Spioenkop.

Here are some steps that the very best agencies and clients do, before they create ads.

*"Now, what do you see?"*

1. Make sure your product, or service is fundamentally sound. That it works and it delivers what you are about to promise in your advertising.

2. If your product or service isn't competitive and doesn't deliver, spend your money and time getting it right before you advertise. If that means training your staff, or hiring new people, or reconfiguring your product, or service offering so it is competitive, do it. There's a saying in the advertising business, the fastest way to ruin a poor product is to advertise it. Remember, you can't use advertising to paper over the cracks of a poor product or service.

3. If you don't have a competitive advantage look for one, or invent one. If it's an emergency service you offer, promise to answer the phone in 3 rings. Or serve your customer, if you own a fast food outlet in 2 minutes, or 20% off their meal. If you serve good food in a no frills restaurant, well that could be a competitive advantage and one you could shout from the rooftops in your advertising ("You pay for the food, not the décor!").

4. Look at what your competitors offer. Go to their web-site (if

they have one) dine in their restaurant, vocal their switchboard, buy or try a sample of their wares, get your friends to try them out…become a secret shopper and see what their strengths and weaknesses are and then determine what yours should be… only then are you good to go, almost.

5. Write yourself a brief. A brief is just that it's a roadmap of what you need to say, to who, and where.

- Who are your competitors?

- What is it, the " Proposition" or "Benefit" that you have that they don't?

- Who is your target market, how old are they, are they male or female or both?

- Where do you think you might "Meet" and entice these people to use your service or product. For example, where do they physically live and shop. Would they read the local paper? Do you think they might listen to a radio station, which one? Would they pick-up a leaflet in a local store?

- What do you want them to do having seen your advertising?

Remember not all advertising needs, or will get an immediate reaction to buy. For example an emergency plumber will only be needed in an emergency, so maybe you want your target audience to write down you name and number, or cut it out from a print advertisement. Or maybe, you want people to come into your store or restaurant on a slow day, a Monday or a Tuesday (and maybe you have a special offer to entice them).

• Lastly, you will need an idea of a budget. How much do you want to invest (not spend, but invest) in reaching your target audience? Don't be afraid to start small, sometimes, even the change of the name of your company, or a change to the design of your business card, or the signage on your company vehicle can and will make a difference to your bottom line. A budget doesn't have to be big, but the thinking has to be right, first.

**OK YOU'RE READY TO CREATE YOUR FIRST PRINT ADVERTISEMENT.**

Out of all the different media available, print, radio, TV, website, outdoor, print advertising is probably where you would start first. You can make it local and it's not so expensive as the other media, excepting your own web site maybe.

First of all remember, no one buys the newspaper or magazine to read the ads…so you are not only competing with other advertisers you are also competing with the editorial. So if you are going to gate crash a party do it with style and engagement.

Moving on from there the first lesson is you are not creating any advertising for yourself; you are creating it for your target audience. So when you judge what you have created be objective and don't ask your wife, friend or colleague if they like it. Chances are they won't want to hurt your feelings and reject the idea you have shown them. If you have to ask their advice ask them how you can improve it!

Your whole ad must create curiosity and impact. This can usually be done with a headline, or a picture,

*Now, have you created curiosity?*

or a combination of both. Or just copy.

The headlines that work best are those that promise a benefit to the reader. Be careful that the benefit is something of benefit to the reader and isn't just a feature of you product. For example, a voucher that offers more airtime isn't a benefit, it's a feature. The benefit is "Talk Longer On Your Cell Phone For Less." Or, "Say hello to more friends this week for free!" We advised a large cell phone company to stop featuring the usual free airtime benefit in the headline and got them to run a consumer benefit line and they increased their income that week by 8 million rand. They ran the ad again and it increased their income to 10 million.

News is also good. If you have news pop into the headline, but don't forget the benefit of that news.

If your advertising in a local paper try putting the name of your location in the headline, people are interested in what is happening where they live.

Pictures can also create great impact. The best pictures are those that engage and arouse the curiosity of your reader.

"Hey, what's happening here they might say," and then read on to find out. Keep the picture simple…all good ads are simple and uncluttered. The more clutter the less focal point there is for the reader to focus on. And, as a general guide, don't put headlines over pictures, they can spoil the headline and they spoil the picture, and chances are the reader won't see either.

Body copy. There is a saying in our industry that everybody is too busy to read body copy nowadays (the text in the advertisement). That isn't true, as I pointed out to one of the misguided Creative Directors at Ogilvy (my old agency) when I showed him some beer ads from the UK that had over 1000 words in them. The ads were packed with information about the beers and they increased the brand's position in the market from 45th in to 5th and increased sales by 29% pa. The brand also picked-up a number of marketing effectiveness awards.

The fact is, you mustn't bore people. People turn their back on bores. Make the body copy interesting and people will read on. If you have a product that you know your customer wants to hear lots about then tell the story, or, if not keep it short and to the point. Pack it with real facts and consumer benefits. Make the sentences short and write them like you would speak them...one human being to another and tell your reader what your product will do for them. Don't brag and boast, no one buys from a bragging loudmouth.

One last thing, your logo doesn't have to be big to gain attention. If people like your ad and what you are saying they will look for the logo and your contact details, just don't make it so small they can't see it though. Generally the best position for your contact details and logo is the bottom right...the eye reads from left to right.

## RADIO - IT HAS GREAT PICTURES

I love writing for radio. Of all the awards I've won, most are for radio. In radio you can really create quite an impact for your brand.

Why?

Well, the secret is there isn't much good radio advertising written because it's not so glitzy as writing for TV, or print or even posters. So if you write and produce good radio it will be heard...and wait for it, be "seen" because good radio is

"Theatre of the Mind," in fact as a young girl said when asked if she preferred radio to TV she said, "radio," because, as she continued "I prefer the pictures on radio!" Her imagination came into play. So can your customer's.

It's a great "Real Time" medium with local relevance too (there are over 200 local stations in many countries) and has the ability to generate immediate awareness of your local business or service. And it's able to reach them, almost wherever they are. In the bath, the bed, car...on the way to the shops, or work. So you can engage with shoppers on their way to the shops. And remember listeners rely on radio for news and often local news, so you can give them your news.

So, how do you do that?

Write radio sparingly. Every word counts, and pauses do too. Pauses arrest the listener; they wonder what is going to be said next. In 30 seconds use no more than 76 words. Ideally less, because...pauses...arrest.

Your spot will have just interrupted the listener's attentions, or it should do, so make sure you do it well. Make sure your spot is, newsy scary, funny, or seductive in the first few seconds other wise the listener will "Tune Out."

Don't waste sound effects either. If you have a sound effect of someone knocking on the door, don't say, "There's a knock at the door, I wonder who it is?" Just say, "Who is it?" after the sound effect of knocking. Every second counts, every second costs money. Don't waste it. Don't have the sound effect of golf ball being hit (and what a cliché that is anyway) and then say, "And there is a golf course nearby to our new estate... " When you could say, "We have all the pleasures and leisure's..." Cut scripts down and make the sound effects paint a picture. Remember it can be "Theatre of the Mind."

If you are writing dialogue, write it as people speak. The ear picks up fake speech.

So absolutely avoid a cacophony of a load of sound effects and a shouting voice or voices. No one buys from anyone who SCREAMS at them. In fact they may well turn the radio off and dislike "you" for SCREAMING at them.

Neither will they hear your message, or find your message

*So, would you buy from a screamer?*

sympathetic if you rush through it at a hundred miles an hour. No one talks that way. So don't.

Find a good voice. Ask the radio producer or radio station to "cast" you a voice for your spot, listen to several and select the most engaging. Ask yourself before you record who is the best voice to represent your product? If you have two voices, make sure you hear what they sound like together. If they complement each other that's great, if they sound the same ditch one and find another.

You might, in some rare cases find that the owner of the business has a great voice for radio. It maybe deep and seductive. Or just very unusual. And unusual is good. Witness the owner of a large retail chain that I had the privilege of working with. He had a strong and unusual foreign accent, slightly hesitant and awkward, and quite frankly supposedly a, "very unprofessional voice." Which it absolutely was. And that is why I, and he had the chutzpah to use him. With great financial and highly amusing effect.

He was in one of his many stores checking out how things were going and he was standing by the cash till talking to a staff member when a customer walked up to him, tapped him on the shoulder and said, in quite a belligerent manner, "Are you the owner of the stores?" To which the managing director replied, "Yes."

Then the conversation went on: -

"Yes I thought you were. It's your voice."

"Yep?"

"Well my daughter, who is an English Graduate, has written to the radio station numerous of times and said you can't speak proper English."

"She has, has she?"

"And she says you should get a proper professional voice to do your radio spots for you… and a proper professional writer."

"She has, has she?"

"And I agree with her. Your voice is quite awful. "

"Yes, my voice is quite awful."

And your radio adverts are awful too. No one would listen to them."

"They wouldn't, would they?"

"No, they wouldn't."

Then the managing director and owner, rocked back on his feet, smiled and burst out in uncontrollable laughter.

"Why are you laughing," said the father of the English Graduate.

"Well look at you!"

"What? What's so funny?"

"Well, you're in my store aren't you? And your trolley, look at your trolley, it's full to the brim with my goods!" 🤑

The bemused customer looked at his trolley laden with goods.

"I rest my case," said the managing director and owner, "My commercials work. You and all those other customers are here aren't you?"

The customer nodded in defeat and burst out laughing as well. And my client laughed all the way to the bank. Sales were up 30% on the previous year…whilst some of his competitors were going to the wall as well.

Lesson learnt. Unusual voice. Honest script. Attract the ears and wallets of the customers.

And hey, don't religiously stick to your script either. If the voice artist (or the managing director, with an unusual accent, in this case) has another way of saying it, try it. Whatever sounds better, or more natural, or makes more sense, use it.

And, please, please, don't just chuck in phone number at the end expecting the listener to get it, they won't. No one is waiting with pen and paper to write down your number. If you are asking them to write down an important number make the whole commercial about that. "At the end of this commercial we are going to give you an important number (or our website address) that its going to save you a lot of money (or could change your life, or give you much pleasure etc)...so (pause) get a pen and paper...are you ready? Ok now...." Or try, "Numbers can change your life, the number of kids you have, the number on your salary cheque, the number 13. Now, at the end of this commercial I'm going to give you a number that could save you bucks...." Don't be afraid of repeating that number throughout your commercial as well.

Lastly, please, don't do jingles. The only person who knows what the sung lyrics are is probably you. They just add to the cacophony of bad commercials. Jingles are old and sad, from the past, and belong there.

Good luck, and enjoy your radio. If you don't, no one else will!

# BILLBOARDS

The first rule of Billboard advertising is blindingly obvious, like any advertising, is "to be seen."

## BILLBOARDS. GLORIOUS IMPACT!

The first rule of Billboard advertising is blindingly obvious, like any advertising, is "to be seen."

And that means first of all buying a billboard that can be seen, by cars hurtling past at least 60kph, or if you are buying a site or sites in a pedestrian area that the pedestrian's can see them.

Check the sites out first. And my advice is don't buy anything on a highway. Can the drivers of the cars stand a chance of seeing your message? And if they are captivated by your message they will probably hit the car in front. Personally, I think all outdoor on roads should be banned. Ah well, I guess it's another income stream for the municipality! Just like cops hiding in he bushes to nab speedsters, instead of policing the roads, billboards on highways should be a no, no.

That may sound so obvious but look at the street pole advertising we see on the roads. Do you think anyone has a chance of reading them as they hurtle by? Check it out next time you are driving. A sobering thought, most of it is crap and won't be seen. Don't waste your money on sites that can't be seen. Be very selective.

So having selected your site another recurring theme comes up. Above all, "Simplicity."

Posters are ideal for creating impact and awareness for your brand or company. So posters, to have impact, need to be simple. As a rule of thumb, no more than 7 to 11 words, and make the type BIG and CAPTIVATE your audience. Your headline must ARREST the consumer, or your visual must arrest them. The rule is, keep it simple. Eliminate, eliminate, eliminate. Remove all the non-essentials the clutter. Keep it clean and simple.

ALWAYS pop your logo in the bottom right of the poster. Why? Because people's eyes are trained to read left to right and down to the left...yes I know you see posters with logo at the top... guess what they have NOT been created by professionals.

Don't feature a phone number unless it's a simple number, easily memorized. Who goes past a poster with a pen and paper ready to take that number! No one.

Here are some headlines that grab attention, "A Wolf In Sheep's Clothing" (for a very sporty saloon car.) "Air is what makes it good" (for a sport's shoe brand). "Life is harsh. Your tequila

Billboards give your brand **IMPACT** and **AWARENESS**.
Make 'em **PUNCH** their **WEIGHT!**

shouldn't be" (picture of Sauva Tequila bottle lying on its side). "A session with us an you'll be able to open any jar" (next to big imposing difficult to open pickle jar and logo of local gym.) "Karate for beginners" (next to broken match stick and logo of the local gym.) Here are some visuals that grab attention, a big close-up of a women's breasts in a bra. In one side a pack of Icebreaker Chewing gum is pushed into the bra, the nipple on the same side is hard and pert, there is no headline. The visual says it all, Icebreaker Gum is very cold! And lastly, a picture of a man with 5 babies, all obviously his, bottom left, Guinness logo and "It's got to be Guinness."

Good luck. Simple is best and simple is seen.

*It was a poster like this that attracted hundreds to a local gym*

**SO, YOU THINK YOU WANT TO BE ON TV?**

First a few words of warning DON'T even consider going on TV unless you have the BUCK$$$$$$$$ to do so. And bucks are split two ways: - the bucks to make the commercial and bucks to flight it, or put it on air. Usually your production budget should be around 10-15% of your airtime budget.

Although it isn't always the case you'll need around R2.5m at the very, very least. And that would need to be used over a very short period to gain any impact.

Fortunately you can, as a "First Time Advertiser" (if you are) get a good discounted rate for airtime.

First, the usual rule applies, as it does for most advertising, IMPACT. If you are writing for TV you need to create a spot that starts with a big bang. A visual, or audio "bang" that makes the viewer sit-up and pay attention. This is particularly true of 10 and 15 second spots. You have no time for a story, or a build-up, as you would for a 30 second or longer.

Always write to the budget. And it doesn't mean, if you have small budget you can't have great impact. I recommend you go onto YouTube and browse the ads for insight and inspiration. It's amazing what you can do with a great script, one actor, a chair and a table. Director Joe Sedelmaier produced some outstanding work, using just this formula.

If I have little money when I write a spot, I start off with, "OK Aubrey, you have no money, a simple set-up and one actor. What can you do with them for the brand?" Then I write within that constraint. Sometimes, I will venture outside that constraint... and maybe find I've got another actor to "play" with, and a voice over. But remember the more you put in, the more it will cost and the more cluttered the commercial will be. Keep it simple, LESS is MORE. (Trust me, in my early days the commercials I wrote were rubbish... because I, or my clients over complicated them, too many words, too many people, too many product benefits, too many scenes, too many cuts, too many problems and too much for the viewer to take in). Cull and cut your script and the contents, and props of your commercial right down.

And dialogue, if that's what your spot is about, create dialogue gaps, as we spoke about in radio ambush your viewer... pauses... in dialogue are great.

If your product can be easily demonstrated, nothing beats a "demo" on TV. They work, but the real trick is to produce them in an unexpected and memorable way. The original Super Glue commercial comes to mind when they stuck a fat man, upside down, on the ceiling with a drop of Super Glue on each shoe. Easy to shoot, no expensive location, no real acting ability required and just a voice over and a pack shot at the end.

Casting, one way you can gain impact is your cast. If you need to cast someone (and chances are, if it's low budget you'll only have "one" someone) make sure that that person can not only do what you want them to do, or say what you want them to say, they can do it in an interesting and ENGAGING way. Look for an oddball. If the script you've written says "Businessman" make sure you go outside the normal cliché box. Find a fat one, or a very tall, or thin and tiny one, someone who will gain the viewers attention. Dress them in an UNUSUAL way for greater impact.

If you want to shoot the commercial yourself I advise you to seriously reconsider, unless you know you can shoot and

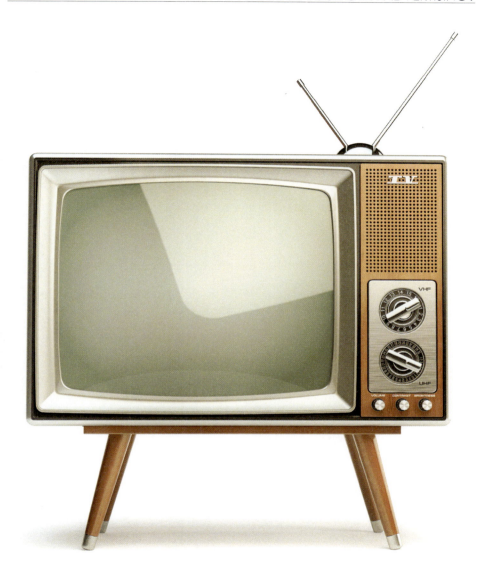

*What are you going to put on TV? Be different and be engaging.*
*Try using an interesting character and you will be seen.*
*Being boring will always lead to failure.*

produce it, and make it to the right technical specification. Making movies is not easy. BEWARE.

If your script is really great you may find a top-class director, or a young aspiring director who wants some great work for their show reel. However this will still cost you. Alternatively you could also find a Director of Photography, or a professional cameraman, who can help shoot the commercial for you. But whatever you do, before you even consider them, look at their show reel first, discuss your idea with them in depth, make absolutely sure you TRUST them…you are about to commit, by anyone's standards, a large amount of money…

## SHOULD YOU HAVE A SLOGAN?

There's controversy over this one in our business. And the answer to the question, "Should I have a slogan" is simple, "Yes" and "No."

"Yes" if it adds value to your offering and "No" when it doesn't, like when it's a cliché, or sounds great but means nothing. Like, "It's only natural" for a Natural Food Company…it's a redundant cliché. Or, "We care" for a pharmaceutical company-I would hope they would care! Or, "Expertise you can trust" for a hospital group, my g*d, I would hope I could trust them. The very fact that they say "Expertise" and "Trust" makes me distrust them a bit already! Besides who likes a bragger? So don't brag or swagger with your slogan.

As a thought, it's worth considering writing a slogan that summarizes what your product, brand or company is about and what makes it different, or why it is different. Here are some examples, " Why Slow Mow when you can Flymo"- who else can own that line? And it has a benefit in it too! "The world's favourite airline," it conjures up all the things you want from a trip in a plane, big, lots of people fly with it, it's safe." I suppose you could have taken an example from the pharmaceutical boys above and written, "Where safety comes first"! I think not.

Here's another, "Good food costs less at Sainsbury's," this line propelled this supermarket chain forward in the UK; it was a succinct and truthful underlining of the benefit of shopping at Sainsbury's. Maybe some of our supermarkets could learn a lesson from that line and stop their bragging? Get down to

# "THE COMPANY YOU CAN TRUST"

(I think not)

earth, we want good food at a good price, don't we?

Here's one for an instant pasta that cooks in 5 minutes, "Just 15 minutes ahead of its time."

And here's my favourite line, for the Victoria and Albert Museum in London, but before I give it to you, and you can appraise it, put yourself in the shoes of the public who will see the slogan. They would be thinking something like this, "Museums are an adventure, crammed full of great stuff but they are generally old fashioned and if I want somewhere to refresh myself they usually have poor quality cafes and coffee shops. Yes I know the Victoria and Albert is a great museum but..." Here's the line that turns all that around, in a most inviting manner, "An ace café, with quite a nice museum attached." Brilliant. The cafés are "ace" and the museum is of course, as we all know, world class (so no need to repeat that in their line)! Great line. Packed museum. Packed Cafes. Job done.

So, as they say in closing, my opinion is better to have none at all, rather than some wimpy line that wants to make the reader vomit, or pass your ad by. Breathe life into your slogan by breathing in the reality of your offer.

# WHERE IS IT ALL GOING TO END?

The greenhouse effect is with us. But there's another effect hitting us too. The intelligence effect.

It's called information. And today we are blessed with buckets of it. We all have access to it and if we bother to use it correctly, it makes us smarter and saves money as well.

The industry has, for a long time now, had media planning information by the yard, but now a new dimension has arrived. Or at least, just the tip of it has arrived and is being used. Today there are massive amounts of information about consumers.

But the problem is, is the industry spending the time to dig, really dig, into the data? As Procter & Gamble have discovered, strategists, real strategists are few and far between. Maybe because agencies' margins are being squeezed and time is at a premium, a cursory look at the data is all that is done. Who's responsible for this? Clients? Yes, some certainly. They won't pay for the data to be bought in the first place. And, if it is being bought, then they won't pay the agency to analyse the data. On the other hand it's the agencies too. To manipulate the data, to dig, they require strategists of the highest calibre. They are few and far between. The ideal combination is someone with a love of figures, economics, trends and also someone who is creative, enquiring, audacious and pioneering. An unusual combination. A bit like a fund manager and creative director rolled into one. Added to this, some creative people - the writers and art directors - don't like insights guiding them, so strategists are seen as, "A waste of skin", as one arrogant creative director pointed out.

*Insights are something you have to dig for - to mine.*

Coupled with this, some clients don't want data to upset the status quo. Trailblazing insights challenge the existing thinking, and unfortunately those who don't embrace the thought of new and challenging insights can get their backsides burnt along the way. So, consciously or subconsciously, they avoid the desire to dig. Better keep the unknown buried rather than unearth a few new roots that can give the brands a stronger foothold in the market.

## CAN YOU PAINT A PICTURE OF YOUR CUSTOMER?

Target Market Index (TGI) has arrived in South Africa. Already available in some 60 countries around the world, TGI is a veritable mine of nourishing and often provocative information. It is a continuous survey of consumer usage habits of brands and media and also covers consumers' attitudes to life, the country, their shopping habits and so on. Digging and delving into TGI will help you paint a portrait of your customer and your competitors' customer. It paints a picture of their characteristics and points you towards potential strategies that can win you new customers, and retain your existing customers. Both agencies and clients use TGI extensively to help them develop more efficient marketing strategies and advertising campaigns. Clients can also use it to look for new outlets for their brands and to see where the growth patterns are and where else consumers of their brands shop.

The consumer sample base is the largest in South Africa (15,000 respondents), and covers the full range of consumer products and services, providing data on some 7000 brands in over 500 product categories, from food, to motoring, financial, retail, sport and leisure, pet and pet foods and personal care.

In short, you would be a fool not to look at the data.

We have used it to help increase the sale of beer by 29% per annum, to find a new point of retail distribution for a brand that now cannot keep up with demand in the new retail outlet, and to isolate the affinity a target group had with a particular medium and therefore increase the brand's sales by a whopping 28%.

TGI data can be bought by subscription, which gives you access to the full amount of mind-blowing data, or you can cherry-pick various reports, tailor-made to your specifications. For example, with the help of the TGI researchers and strategists you can look at every nook and cranny relating to your and your competitors' brands. The interactive sessions allow you to test various hypotheses and analyse trends and consumption patterns. Alternatively you can commission a quick view of your brand's performance, look at users and non-users, frequency of use, demographics, and (far more useful and enormously stimulating), psychographics, as well as geodemographics, life values of your customers and so on (www.tgi.co.za).

Building brands and nurturing them is an ongoing and fascinating process. It requires constant attention and review. Challenging thinking. Above all, it requires a consistent and cohesive strategy and rigid adherence to the values of the brands and the tone and manner we choose to use. Brands can be killed quickly by foolish thinking but they are not built overnight. As the saying goes:

*"A drop of rain maketh a hole in the stone, not by violence, but by oft falling."*

*Hugh Latimer.*

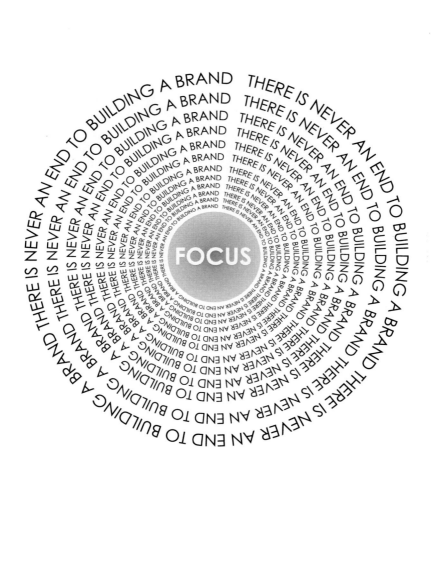

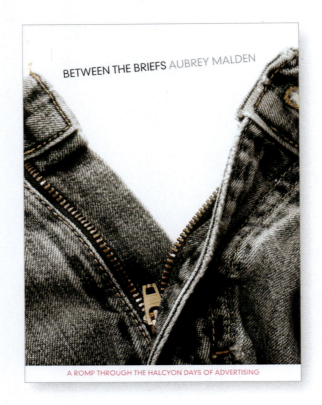

BETWEEN THE BRIEFS AUBREY MALDEN

A ROMP THROUGH THE HALCYON DAYS OF ADVERTISING

# OTHER BOOKS BY THE AUTHOR

"MADE ME *LAUGH A LOT*"
"*PRECIOUS*...WORTH PRESERVING"
"TARTS IN CANNES. IT'S A *SHOCKER!*"
"*BRILLIANTLY* TOLD"
"*WITTY*...DELIGHTFUL STORIES"

ISBN • 978-0-620-67626-7